Hymns of the Apostolic Church

By Rev. John Brownlie, D.D.
This Edition Edited by Anthony Uyl

Woodstock, Ontario, Canada 2018

Hymns of the Apostolic Church
Hymns of the Apostolic Church
Being Centos and Suggestions from the Service Books of the Holy Eastern Church
with Introduction and Historical and Biographical Notes by the Rev. John Brownlie, D.D.
This Edition Edited by Anthony Uyl

Originally Published by:
Paisley: Alexander Gardner, Publisher by Appointment to the late Queen Victoria 1909

The text of Hymns of the Apostolic Church is all in the Public Domain. The layout and Devoted Publishing logo are Copyright ©2018 Devoted Publishing. This edition is published by Devoted Publishing a division of 2165467 Ontario Inc.

What kind of philosophies do you have?
Let us know!

Visit our website: www.devotedpublishing.com
Contact us at: devotedpub@hotmail.com
Visit us on Facebook: @DevotedPublishing

Published in Woodstock, Ontario, Canada 2018.

For bulk educational rates, please contact us at the above email address.

ISBN: 978-1-77356-243-8

Table of Contents

INTRODUCTION 5
   HYMNALS COLLATED 8
BIOGRAPHICAL AND HISTORICAL 12
Hymns of the Apostolic Church . 18
   INFINITE GOD 18
   MORNING I 20
   MORNING II 21
   MORNING III 23
   MORNING IV 24
   MORNING V 25
   MORNING VI 26
   MORNING VII 27
   EVENING I 28
   EVENING II 30
   EVENING III 32
   EVENING IV 33
   ADVENT AND CHRISTMAS I 34
   ADVENT AND CHRISTMAS II 35
   ADVENT AND CHRISTMAS III 37
   PASSIONTIDE AND EASTER I 39
   PASSIONTIDE AND EASTER II 40
   PASSIONTIDE AND EASTER III 41
   PASSIONTIDE AND EASTER IV 42
   PASSIONTIDE AND EASTER V 43
   PASSIONTIDE AND EASTER VI 44

Rev. John Brownlie, D.D.

   PASSIONTIDE AND EASTER VII 46
   PASSIONTIDE AND EASTER VIII 47
   PASSIONTIDE AND EASTER IX 49
   PASSIONTIDE AND EASTER X 50
   PASSIONTIDE AND EASTER XI 51
   PASSIONTIDE AND EASTER XII 52
   PASSIONTIDE AND EASTER XIII 53
   PASSIONTIDE AND EASTER XIV 54
   PASSIONTIDE AND EASTER XV 56
   PASSIONTIDE AND EASTER XVI 57
   PASSIONTIDE AND EASTER XVII 59
   ASCENSION I 61
   ASCENSION II 62
   ASCENSION III 63
   ASCENSION IV 64
   ASCENSION V 65
   PENTECOST I 66
   PENTECOST II 67
   PENTECOST III 69
   PENTECOST IV 70
   PENTECOST V 71
   JUDGMENT I 72
   JUDGMENT II 74
   JUDGMENT III 76

JUDGMENT IV 77	MEDITATIONS XI 95
VICTORY I 78	MEDITATIONS XII 96
VICTORY II 79	MEDITATIONS XIII 98
VICTORY III 81	MEDITATIONS XIV 99
VICTORY IV 82	MEDITATIONS XV 100
MEDITATIONS I 83	MEDITATIONS XVI 101
MEDITATIONS II 84	VARIOUS I 102
MEDITATIONS III 85	VARIOUS II 104
MEDITATIONS IV 86	VARIOUS III 106
MEDITATIONS V 87	VARIOUS IV 107
MEDITATIONS VI 88	VARIOUS V 108
MEDITATIONS VII 89	VARIOUS VI 109
MEDITATIONS VIII 90	VARIOUS VII 110
MEDITATIONS IX 92	VARIOUS VIII 112
MEDITATIONS X 94	APPENDIX 113

Rev. John Brownlie, D.D.

INTRODUCTION

Yet another series of hymns from the Greek Office Books. Some of them are translations or renderings, more are centos, but most are suggestions, or based upon the Greek. To quote from the author's preface to his third series:-- "In process of reading, thoughts linked themselves to the memory, and echoes of music--much of it surpassingly sweet--lingered, and from those echoes and thoughts the centos and suggestions have been formed. The phrases containing the thoughts, and the echoes repeating the music, have been woven together to form the fabric which is shown here." And again, from the Introduction to his fourth series:--"The Greek has been used as a basis, a theme, a motive; oriental colour, and, it is to be hoped, some of the oriental warmth, has been preserved. Now and again an oriental figure is retained, and to those who have any knowledge of the worship of the Eastern Church, it must be obvious that the peculiar themes of her praise are in abundant evidence." These extracts accurately describe the contents of the greater part of this volume.

It is in their suggestiveness that the chief attraction of Greek hymns lies. By the ordinary process of translation a hymn is reproduced in its excessive symbolism and multiplicity of metaphor, and the result in our matter-of-fact language is incongruity. The harmony which it presents in the original language and setting, and the combined effect of symbol and metaphor, are in most cases lost, and discord is the result. It is by capturing the subtle suggestion of the original, and utilising it to the best advantage, that the value of the Greek hymn is made appreciable. That this is the general conviction is evidenced by the fact that none of Dr. Neale's work is so popular, and rightly so, as the hymns, "Art thou weary, art thou languid?" and "O happy band of pilgrims," and neither of these hymns is a translation: both are merely suggestions from the Greek.

In no hymns is this suggestiveness more felt than in those for the morning and evening, which are found in many of the Offices. The Greek hymn writers took time to watch the sun rise and set. The glow of early dawn spreading and brightening; the clouds fringed with purple and gold; the glowing shafts chasing the retreating darkness--this morning vision awakened in them thoughts which have inspired meditative minds in all ages, but which it is enriching to have expressed in the peculiarly suggestive manner of the Greek Christian poet. As with the sunrise, so with the sunset. The morning and evening give buoyancy and restfulness to Greek hymnody, and clothe the work of its choicest singers with a brightness and varying beauty which are the abiding characteristics of those seasons.

But if one would realise in the greatest possible degree the wealth of Greek praise, he must acquaint himself with the Offices for Passiontide and Easter, as they are contained in the Triodion and Pentecostarion. There the Christ, in all the humiliation of His manhood, bearing the burden of fallen humanity to the Cross, is presented to us in a guise, if not attractive, certainly fascinating and pregnant in suggestion; while the Resurrection victory is proclaimed in Easter song in tones the gladdest, sweetest, and most triumphant in the whole range of Greek hymnody; for it is in Easter song that the Greek Church excels.

By its objectiveness, the Greek hymn enables us to do for ourselves what our less wholesome subjective hymns aim at doing for us, and not always successfully. It presents the picture, and if the worshipper be not hopelessly blind, he sees it, and the impression is made upon the mind and heart, with the desired result in varying degrees. It is this that makes the Greek hymn so suggestive. Hence it is that the hymn which is the result of a reminiscence of the Greek is usually subjective. We are under no temptation to reproduce the writer's words and figures. The outline fades, but the impression remains and possesses the mind, and it is that that is given. So there is inspiration in Greek hymnody for every mind capable of inspiration.

What we cannot understand is that this treasure-house of song, and of inspiration to singing, should be so persistently ignored, and should still attract so few capable workers. Practically it remains almost unexplored, notwithstanding that enough has been brought to light to awake desire for more. Had we treated the hymnody of the Latin Church, and the Church of the Reformation in Germany, after this fashion, our praise would have suffered incalculably. But we have made the praise of those Churches our own, by the work of a band of devoted translators, while practically ignoring that of the Church of the Apostles. The present writer, in his Introduction to The Hymns of the Holy Eastern Church, has suggested a few possible causes of this state of matters, but none of them is sufficient, nor all of them combined. When once we overcome our indifference to a great past to which we owe so much, and disabuse our minds of an uncatholic localism, an interest in the Church of the East and her worship will possess us--but not till then. We want hymn writers of the first rank, who have the necessary knowledge of the language, to venture into the unexplored region, to cull its choicest flowers, and bring them back to adorn the temple of the Living God; and, fired with the inspiration which a sojourn there must give, to send forth in new dress and fresh attractiveness the glorious truths which are the possession of the Church of God in all ages, but which our modern hymnody is in danger of reiterating with stale monotony.

From the Table which the author has been at the trouble to prepare, it will be seen that there are only forty-one hymns from the Greek in common use. The blame for such a deplorable condition of things lies at the door of the Christian Church of our time, which has failed, by its hymn writers who had the needful equipment, to make those hymns available to a greater extent; and partly at the door of compilers of hymnals, who have not sufficiently made use of the material which is available.

What, then, are the available sources when compilers ask for Greek hymns for their compilations? The first really masterly contribution to our English hymnody from Greek sources was that made by Dr. Neale. With his work as a whole in relation to the Greek Church, we have nothing to do here. Early attracted to the Greek Office Books, he set himself to introduce the hymns with which they are embellished to the notice of his fellow-countrymen. So well was his task performed, that in a very short time the best of them were appropriated by the Church for her praise, and to the present day they hold a secure place in all our best hymnals. In 1862, he published Hymns of the Eastern Church, which contains about sixty pieces--his complete contribution to English hymnody from the Greek, and a very substantial contribution indeed, far surpassing anything that has been done until very recently. About the same time, or a little later, Dr. Littledale drew the attention of the Church to the Greek Offices by his Offices from the Service Books of the Holy Eastern Church (1863), and he also prepared a few metrical translations of hymns, which may be found in The People's Hymnal (1867). Dr. Littledale's renderings--which are, needless to say, very true--are in most cases graceful and winning, and do not deserve the neglect which they have suffered. Mr. W. Chatterton Dix, a considerable name in hymnody, would seem to have been stirred to follow the pioneers as closely as possible; for while he made no entirely original contribution from the Greek, he worked upon some of Dr. Littledale's prose translations, putting them into graceful metrical form. This he did to a considerable extent, but the result is, as might be anticipated, artificial, and lacking the spirit which a thorough acquaintance with the original alone can give. Mr. Dix's work can be seen in the Lyra Messianica (1865), where about a dozen of his metrical renderings find a place. These, too, have all been allowed to lie unused. The Rev. Allen W. Chatfield did good service by rendering much of the poetry of the early Greek Christian poets, which had been compiled by MM. Christ and Paranikas (Anthologia Graeca Carminum Christianorum, 1871). The hymns in that collection are not found in the Greek Service Books, with the exception of a few by St. John of Damascus; but from the renderings which were made by Mr. Chatfield, and published by him in 1876 under the title, Songs and Hymns of the Earliest Greek Christian Poets, Bishops, and Others, a few very beautiful centos have been formed, notably one beginning "Lord Jesus, think on me," which has been included in no fewer than five permanent hymnals, as may be seen from the Table. The Rev. Gerald Moultrie, who prepared renderings from several languages, contributed a few from the Greek, but only a few. The best is his rendering of the midnight hymn, "Behold, the Bridegroom cometh in the middle of the night." From that time till now, very little attention has been given to the Greek Offices, until we come to the Rev. R. M. Moorsom, whose intensely catholic instincts led him to use the gift he possessed in the service of the praise of the Church, to which he contributed twenty-two pieces from eastern sources--Renderings of Church Hymns (1901). Two of these have already found a place in the revised edition of Church Hymns (1903) and of Hymns Ancient and Modern (1904). In the recently published English Hymnal, three new names of translators from the Greek are to be found--Rev. T. A. Lacey, Mr. Athelstan Riley, and Mr. C. W. Humphreys. Their contributions are few, but we do not know to what extent they may yet pursue the work.

    Giving the most generous estimate, there could not, till very recently, have been more than 150 hymns from the Greek available for the use of compilers of hymnals. To that number, however, are now to be added 108 translations and 153 centos and suggestions by the present author--261 pieces in all. That work of this kind is welcomed and readily appropriated, is evidenced by the fact that, although his first series was published so recently as eight years ago, several of the hymns have been included in most of the hymnals compiled or revised since then, both in this country and in America.

    The Table will show at a glance to what extent available material has been taken advantage of by hymnal compilers. The twelve principal hymnals compiled or revised since 1892 have been collated, and the Greek hymns contained in each set forth. It will be seen that there are only forty-one of these hymns in common use. A gratifying feature is that the most recently prepared collections contain the greatest number. The Methodist Hymn Book contains four--the smallest number; The English Hymnal, twenty-four--the greatest number. The most popular hymns of the forty-one are, "Art thou weary?" and "The day is past and over," which are included in all the twelve hymnals; and "O happy band of pilgrims" and "The day of Resurrection," which appear in eleven and nine of the twelve respectively. A noteworthy circumstance, as already stated, is that two of the most popular hymns are not renderings in the proper sense, but merely suggestions--"Art thou weary?" and "O happy band of pilgrims"--an indication of the direction in which successful effort must be made in dealing with Greek hymnody by those competent to do so.

HYMNALS COLLATED

A. The Hymnal (Episcopal Church, U.S.A.), 1892.
B. The Hymnal (Presbyterian Church, U.S.A.), 1895.
C. The Presbyterian Book of Praise (Canada), 1897.
D. The Church Hymnary (Presby., Scotland), 1898.
E. Baptist Church Hymnal, 1900.
F. Church Hymns, 1903.
G. Hymns Ancient and Modern, 1904.
H. The Methodist Hymn Book, 1904.
I. New Office Hymn Book, 1905.
K. Worship Song (Congregational), 1905.
L. English Hymnal, 1906.
M. Church Praise (English Presbyterian), 1908.

First Lines HYMNALS
A B C D E F G H I K L M
1. A great and mighty wonder
(St. Anatolius, 8th century) tr. Dr. Neale,
... ... 1 ... 1 ... 2
2. Art thou weary, art thou languid?
(Based upon the Greek) tr. Dr. Neale,
1 1 1 1 1 1 1 1 1 1 1 12
3. Behold, the bridegroom cometh
(Midnight Office) tr. G. Moultrie,
... ... 1 1 ... 2
4. Behold, the bridegroom draweth nigh
(Midnight Office) tr. R. M. Moorsom,
... ... 1 1 2
5. Christian, dost thou see them?
(St. Andrew of Crete, 600-732) tr. Dr. Neale,
1 ... ... 1 ... 1 ... 1 1 5
6. Close beside the heart that loves me
(Based upon the Greek) tr. Dr. Brownlie,
... ... 1 1
7. Come, ye faithful, raise the strain
(St. John Damascene, c. 780) tr. Dr. Neale,

Rev. John Brownlie, D.D.

1 1 ... ... 1 1 ... 1 ... 1 ... 6
8. Far from Thy heavenly care
(St. Joseph of the Studium, 9th century) tr. Dr Brownlie,
... ... 1 1
9. Fierce was the wild billow
(St. Anatolius) tr. Dr. Neale,
... 1 1 ... 1 1 ... ... 1 ... 1 1 7
10. From glory to glory advancing
(Liturgy of St. James) tr. C. W. Humphreys,
... ... 1 ... 1
11. God of all grace, Thy mercy send
(Litany of the Deacon) tr. Dr. Brownlie,
... ... 1 ... ... 1 ... 2
12. Hail, gladdening Light
(Sophronius? 7th century) tr. John Keble,
... ... 1 ... 1 1 ... 1 ... ... 1 5
13. In days of old on Sinai
(St. Cosmas, c. 760) tr. Dr. Neale,
... ... 1 1
14. Jesus, name all names above
(St. Theoctistus, c. 890) tr. Dr. Neale,
... ... 1 ... ... 1 ... 2
15. Lead, Holy Shepherd, lead us
(St. Clement, b.c. 170) tr. Dr. H. M'Gill,
... ... 1 1 2
16. Let all mortal flesh keep silence
(Liturgy of St. James) tr. G. Moultrie,
... ... 1 ... 1
17. Let our choir new anthems raise
(St. Joseph of the Studium) tr. Dr. Neale,
... ... 1 1 ... 1 ... 1 ... 4
18. Lord Jesus, think on me
(Synesius, 375-430) tr. A. W. Chatfield,
1 ... ... 1 1 ... 1 ... 1 ... 5
19. Lord, to our humble prayers attend
(The Great Collect) tr. Dr. Brownlie,
... ... 1 ... ... 1 ... 1 ... 3
20. O brightness of the Eternal Father's face
(Sophronius?) tr. E. W. Eddis,
1 ... ... 1 2
21. O Gladsome Light, O Grace
(Sophronius?) tr. R. B.,
... ... 1 ... 1
22. O happy band of pilgrims
(Based upon the Greek) tr. Dr. Neale,
1 1 1 1 1 1 ... 1 1 1 1 11
23. O king enthroned on high
(Office for Pentecost) tr. Dr. Brownlie,
... ... 1 ... ... 1 ... 1 ... 3
24. O Light that knew no dawn

Hymns of the Apostolic Church
(St. Gregory, 325) tr. Dr. Brownlie,
... ... 1 ... ... 1 2
25. O the Mystery, passing wonder
(St. Andrew of Crete) tr. Dr. Neale,
... ... 1 1
26. O Unity of three-fold light
(Metrophanes of Smyrna, 6th century) tr. Dr. Neale,
... ... 1 ... 1
27. O Word Immortal of Eternal God
(Emperor Justinian, 6th century) tr. T. A. Lacey,
... ... 1 ... 1
28. O Word of God, in devious paths
(St. Gregory) tr. Dr. Brownlie,
... ... 1 1
29. Safe home, safe home in port
(Based upon the Greek) tr. Dr. Neale,
... ... 1 ... ... 1 2
30. Shepherd of tender youth
(Clement of Alexandria) tr. H. M. Dexter,
1 1 ... ... 1 3
31. Stars of the morning, so gloriously bright
(St. Joseph) tr. Dr. Neale,
1 ... ... 1 1 ... 1 ... 1 ... 5
32. Sweet Saviour, in Thy pitying grace
(St. Theoctistus) tr. R. M. Moorsom,
... ... 1 1 2
33. The day of Resurrection
(St. John Damascene) tr. Dr. Neale,
1 1 ... 1 ... ... 1 1 1 1 1 1 9
34. The day is past and over
(St. Anatolius) tr. Dr. Neale,
1 1 1 1 1 1 1 1 1 1 1 1 12
35. The Lord and King of all things
(St. Anatolius) tr. Dr. Neale,
... ... 1 ... 1
36. Those eternal bowers
(St. John Damascene) tr. Dr. Neale,
1 ... 1 1 ... ... 1 ... 1 5
37. Thou hallowed, chosen morn of praise
(St. John Damascene) tr. Dr. Neale,
... ... 1 ... 1
38. Thou, Lord, hast power to heal
(Order of Holy Unction) tr. Dr. Brownlie,
... ... 1 ... 1
39. What shall we bring to Thee?
(St. Anatolius) tr. Dr. Brownlie,
... ... 1 1
40. What sweet of life endureth
(St. John Damascene) tr. A. Riley,
... ... 1 ... 1

Rev. John Brownlie, D.D.

41. When Thou shalt come, O Lord
(Morning, Sexagesima Sunday) tr. Dr. Brownlie,
... ... 1 1
11 7 6 7 6 17 14 4 21 6 24 8 13 1

    Is it too much to hope for, in the interests of congregational praise, that more attention will be given to the contents of the Greek Office Books in the future than has been given to them in the past? But intending students must have ready access to them. Where are they to be found? Unless it is resolved to purchase them, which may be done through a bookseller in Athens or Constantinople, search will probably be made for them in vain in our libraries. They are to be found in the Bodleian Library, and in the library of St. John's College, Oxford, and also in the library of Cambridge University; but it is doubtful if the library of any other university or theological school in England possesses them. We, in Scotland, are even less fortunate. A year ago, the writer was unaware of the existence of a set of the Greek Service Books, other than his own, in Scotland. Last year, the Library Committee of Glasgow University purchased a complete set, and her students may now acquaint themselves with the contents as they feel inclined. Will Edinburgh, St. Andrews, and Aberdeen follow the example of Glasgow? And will our theological schools do the same? And when that has been done, will our professors of theology suggest to their students that it might be worth their while to dip into their contents? In this way, the fact of the existence of these books would be kept before the minds of those from whose number interpreters of their hymns are most likely to come, and some hope be reasonably entertained of a growing acquaintance with them as time passes. Meanwhile, the density of ignorance of even well informed men, on the subject of the Greek Church generally, is disheartening, while to our ordinary worshippers it is little more than a name, if even that.

    The hymns in this, and in former volumes, have been prepared in the hope that they may be of service in the public worship of the Three-One God, and hymnal compilers who may be attracted to them, and who may deem them suitable for their purpose, are at liberty to make use of them without the payment of any fee, but on the following simple conditions:--(1) Permission must be asked, and a formal acknowledgment made in the hymnal when published. This is not always done. In a recent case, an historical error was set afoot which may cause future hymnologists some trouble to rectify, and which would certainly have been obviated had this common courtesy been observed. (2) The text of the hymns must not be tampered with in the very slightest particular: they must be printed exactly as they appear in the author's collection. If compilers wish to omit any verse or verses, permission to do so must be asked. (3) The author expects that a copy of the hymnal containing his work will be sent to him on publication.

Trinity Manse,
Portpatrick, Easter, 1909.

BIOGRAPHICAL AND HISTORICAL

The following Notes have reference only to those Hymn Writers of the Greek Church whose work is represented by English versions in the Hymnals collated in the foregoing Table, and which are consequently, to some extent, in common use. They are only twelve in number, and account for thirty of the forty-one hymns. The authorship of the remaining eleven is unknown.

St. Clement of Alexandria

Clemens, Titus Flavius (Clemens Alexandrinus), St. Clement of Alexandria. This remarkable man was born either at Athens or Alexandria, but the exact date of his birth is uncertain. He was a philosopher and theologian, and lived in the end of the second and beginning of the third century. He was well versed in Greek science, and being attracted by the teaching of Christianity, he set himself to investigate its truth. Wherever an exponent of the new religion could be found, Clement sought him out to learn more from his lips. With this end in view, he travelled over Greece, Italy, Egypt, Palestine, and the East. Among all his teachers, he expressly mentions Pantaenus, by whom he was induced to embrace Christianity. When Pantaenus, who was head of the Catechetical School at Alexandria, died, Clement succeeded him as its head, and continued to work there as an exponent of Christianity, from 190 to 203 (?) He attracted numerous pupils, so great was his fame as a teacher, some of whom rose to distinction in later years. Among these may be mentioned Origen, and Alexander who ultimately became Bishop of Jerusalem. When the persecution under Severus broke out, Clement, with others professing the Christian faith, fled. Of his subsequent life very little is known.

A peculiarity of Clement's teaching was that, when he embraced Christianity, he did not abandon his eclectic system of philosophy, afterwards called Neo-Platonism, and always utilized heathen antiquities, when, with their help, he could throw light upon Christian doctrine.

Clement's works are published as part of the Anti-Nicene Christian Library (1867). The one we have to do with here is The Instructor, or Paedagogus, in which he gives advice and instruction on questions of morality. Appended to this work is the poem Stomion polon adaon, which was first translated by Dr. H. M. Dexter in 1846, as "Shepherd of Tender Youth." The original, which is a dithyrambic ode to the Saviour, is a curious production. Here is a literal rendering of the latter part of the ode:--"Guide [us] Shepherd of rational sheep; guide unharmed children, O Holy King, along the footsteps of Christ; O Heavenly Way, Perennial Word, Immeasurable Age, Eternal Light, Fount of Mercy, Performer of Virtue; noble [is the] life of those who hymn God, O Christ Jesus, heavenly milk of the sweet breasts of the graces of the Bride pressed out of Thy wisdom. Babes nourished with tender mouths, filled with the dewy wisdom of the rational pap, let us sing together simple praises, true hymns to Christ [our] King, holy fee for the teaching of life." From this string of epithets several translators have, with remarkable ingenuity, woven very attractive versions.

Clement is interesting to hymnologists as having been the author of this earliest extant versified Christian hymn. He died early in the third century.

St. Gregory Nazianzen

Gregory of Nazianzus, son of Gregory, Bishop of Nazianzus in Cappadocia, and life-long friend of Basil, Bishop of Caesarea, was born at a village near Nazianzus, 325 A.D. He was early taught the truths of Christianity by his mother, and passed into the school of Carterius at Caesarea, who subsequently became the head of the monasteries of Antioch, and teacher of Chrysostom, Bishop of Constantinople. He took up the priestly office at the earnest request of his father, and for some time was helpful to the aged Bishop.

The times in which Gregory lived were trying times. The orthodox Christians clung to the creed of Nicea, and their champions did valiant battle with the Arians. As an advocate and exponent of evangelical truth, Gregory was summoned to Constantinople in 379, and as Bishop of that See, adorned the high office with gifts and graces as brilliant as they were rare. But he was not the man for such a prominent position at a time so eventful. Hilary, the "Hammer of the Arians," could keep the heretics at bay, and accomplish in the Latin Church what Gregory failed to do in the Greek Church--maintain his position and his cause against all comers. For one thing, the retiring disposition of Gregory made him shrink from the din of conflict, and his high ideals weakened his hopefulness. The result was that he abandoned the position, and retired to Nazianzus in 381. Deprived by death of his life-long friend and brother, Caesarius, he retired from the world, and penned those poems, some of which are among the treasures of the Church catholic.

Gregory is better known as a theologian than as a poet, although his verses exceed in number thirty thousand. They are found in the second volume of the Benedictine Edition of his works, which was published in Paris in 1842. A selection can be seen in Daniel's Thesaurus Hymnologicus, and in the Anthologia Graeca, Carminum Christianorum.

Synesius

Synesius was born about 375 A.D. In many particulars he was an outstanding man. His pedigree is said to have extended through seventeen centuries, and to have included the names of the most illustrious. Not only was he of noble lineage, he was also a man of high character and brilliant attainments. He was versed in the Neo-Platonic philosophy, and his Christianity has been called in question by no less an authority than Mosheim; but how anyone can read his odes and doubt the reality of his Christianity, even in the fullest sense of the term as including belief in the Divinity of Christ and in His Resurrection, is difficult to understand. He certainly was a good man, and knew Christ, and loved Him. His writings prove that; and in 410, though reluctantly, he became Bishop of Ptolemais. Very little of his poetry has come down to us, but that little is of the highest order. His hymns are not found in the Greek Offices. He died 430 A.D.

Justinian I

Justinian I. (Flavius Anicius Justinianus), Emperor of the Eastern Roman Empire, was born at Tauresium, the modern Kustenje, on the Black Sea, 11th May, 483 A.D. He was educated at Constantinople, and succeeded his uncle, Justin I., 527. The crowning misfortune of his life was his marriage to Theodora, a professional actress, who, along with Antonina--wife of his friend and victorious general, Belisarius--was responsible for most of the unhappiness of his life. His reign was a most eventful one. His victories over the Persians in the East, and the Goths and Vandals in Italy, were numerous. At the outset of his reign, Justinian was orthodox, but, under the influence of Theodora, he gradually veered round to the monophysite error. It was at her instigation that he attempted to coerce the monophysites into orthodoxy--an attempt which ended in the faction fight of the hippodrome, in which thirty thousand were killed.

Justinian was the founder of that style of architecture called Byzantine, the distinctive features of which are the Greek cross and the cupola. He adorned Constantinople and other cities of his dominions with costly and magnificent churches. In Constantinople alone he built twenty-seven--one of these being St. Sophia, which stands to-day a monument to his enterprise. The St. Sophia of Julian had been destroyed by fire in the insurrection of 532. The re-building occupied six years, and gave work to about ten thousand men, who were paid at the close of each day. It cost the equivalent of £13,000,000. "I have vanquished thee, O Solomon!" was Justinian's pardonable exclamation at its completion.

The crowning glory of Justinian's reign, however, and a lasting monument to his genius, was the Corpus Juris Civilis, or body of civil law, which he executed. By that great work he gave the Roman law, which has formed the groundwork of the civil law of all civilized peoples, a definite code.

Justinian died 565, at the age of eighty-two, having reigned for thirty-eight years. He was a man of great business capacity, resourceful and energetic. He was, moreover, a man of much learning, which he applied to good purpose, but his religious bigotry, and the evil influence of Theodora, marred his good qualities.

The Hymn of Justinian is found in the liturgies of St. Mark and St. James, and is generally attributed to him. Whether he himself composed it, or whether it bears his name for some other reason, there is no means at hand to determine. It is believed to have been his own composition. In a literal translation it runs thus:--

"Only Begotten Son, and Word of God, Immortal Who didst vouchsafe for our salvation to take flesh of the Holy Mother of God and ever Virgin Mary, and didst without change become man, and wast crucified, Christ our God, and by death didst overcome death, being One of the Holy Trinity, and glorified together with the Father and the Holy Ghost, save us."

This hymn has been rendered into English verse, "O Word Immortal of Eternal God," by T. A. Lacey, and appears in The English Hymnal.

Rev. John Brownlie, D.D.

St. Andrew of Crete

St. Andrew of Crete was born 660 A.D., in the city of Damascus. For the reason that he embraced the monastic life at Jerusalem, he is sometimes called St. Andrew of Jerusalem. In his early life he revealed an unchristian lack of decision for truth which has not tended to sweeten his memory. He was raised to the Archiepiscopate of Crete by the usurper Philippicus, called Bardanes, who had been raised to the throne by his army--although he was only its general--after the murder of Justinian II. As Archiepiscopate, he agreed to act as a deputy at the pseudo synod of Constantinople, which met in 712 under the auspices of Philippicus, and there condemned the decisions of the former Council, of which he had been a member. The Monothelite heresy, which taught that our Lord had only one will as He had but one nature, was there restored. Andrew, however, abandoned his error in later life. He died in the island of Hierissus, in the Aegean Sea, about 730 A.D.

To what extent his hymns appear in the Service Books it is difficult to discover. His authorship of certain of the earlier canons is undisputed. He wrote also many Idiomela. His Great Canon, or, as the Greeks delight to term it, "The King of Canons," is in use at Mid Lent. It is an ambitious composition of about three hundred stanzas, in which numerous scriptural examples are used to inspire a spirit of penitence. Some of the stanzas are attractive. Dr. Neale, in his Hymns of the Eastern Church, gives a few from the beginning of the canon. The stichera for Thursday of Holy Week, beginning, "O the Mystery passing wonder," are included in The New Office Hymn Book.

Sophronius

Sophronius was Patriarch of Jerusalem early in the seventh century. Specimens of his poetical work can be seen in the third volume of Daniel's Thesaurus. A few of his Idiomela are found in the Menaea, and also in the Horologion. If we except the hymn rendered by John Keble, "Hail, gladdening Light," and which has been attributed to him--although Athenogenes of Cappadocia, who suffered martyrdom under Diocletian c. A.D. 200, and is said to have sung the hymn while the flames encircled him, shares the honour in the Greek Church--none of his hymns have been translated into English. That hymn, phos hilaron hagias doxes, is quoted by St. Basil in the fourth century, and then as of unknown authorship. The likelihood is, therefore, that it is one of the earliest Christian hymns, possibly of the second century. It is used as a vesper hymn in the Greek Church, and as such finds a place in the Service Books. It has been often translated, and in John Keble's version is one of the best known hymns from the Greek Offices.

St. Anatolius

Very little is known of Anatolius. Dr. Neale gives the date of his death as 458 A.D. In this he is mistaken, and would seem to be identifying him with a patriarch of that name who succeeded Flavius in 449. From the fact that a letter from him exists addressed to Joseph of the Studium (eighth century), and also that he celebrates the martyrs who suffered in the sixth and seventh centuries, his date cannot be earlier than the beginning of the eighth century.

His hymns, which number about one hundred, are found in the Menaea and Octoechus. Several of them were rendered by Dr. Neale, and are included in Hymns of the Eastern Church; and a few by Dr. Littledale can be seen in his Offices of the Holy Eastern Church. "The day is past and over," and "Fierce was the wild billow," are both, in the original, the work of Anatolius, and are well known in their attractive renderings by Dr. Neale.

St. John of Damascus

John of Damascus is by far the most prominent, and most poetical of all the Greek Christian poets. The exact date of his birth is unknown, but he died c. 780 A.D. the last of the theologians of the Greek Church. He dwelt for many years in Damascus, his native city, a valiant champion of orthodoxy against all opponents. His influence on Greek hymnody was immense, and he was held in high esteem by the Greek Church for his work in that department. The Octoechus, which contains the Ferial Office, was largely the work of John. There his canons are found which are perhaps his greatest work in hymnody. The canons under the name of John Arklas are usually attributed to St. John, and also those under the name of John the Monk. John, in company with Cosmas his foster-brother, retired eventually to the monastery of St. Sabas, in Palestine, where he spent a life of devotion, and sang those Christian hymns which have cheered and inspired so many generations of Christians in the East. There he penned the "Golden Canon" for Easter Day, which breathes the glorious hopes of the Resurrection. He lived, it is believed, to extreme old age, dying at the close of the year 780.

St. Cosmas, the Melodist

St. Cosmas, surnamed the Melodist, was foster-brother of John of Damascus, to whom he was attached by closest bonds of friendship. He retired with the famous theologian and hymn writer, to the monastery of St. Sabas, in Palestine, where he spent his leisure in the composition of hymns, many of which found their way, along with those of John of Damascus, into the Greek Offices. There he also shared the work connected with the preparation of The Octoechus with his foster-brother. To what extent his hymns found a place in the Greek Offices, it is difficult to say. If all those bearing his name are accepted as his, then his contribution is a fairly large one. He is represented by canons on The Nativity, The Epiphany, The Transfiguration, and Palm Sunday; also by sundry other pieces. His poetry, although it is said they composed in friendly rivalry, cannot bear comparison with that of St. John, in any particular. It has, however, qualities which claim for it the appreciative reference which Dr. Neale bestows upon it.

Cosmas became Bishop of Maiuma, near Gaza, in 743, and died about 760. He is commemorated by the Greek Church on October 14th.

St. Joseph of the Studium

Joseph of the Studium, sometimes designated The Hymnographer, was born on the island of Sicily, in the end of the eighth century, or the beginning of the ninth. It has been disputed whether indeed the double designation belongs to one person. Into that question we have no occasion to enter here. Up to the present time we have had no evidence to prove that the Hymnographer was not of the Studium, and that the hymns of St. Joseph, which are so much in evidence in the Service Books, are not the work of one writer.

St. Joseph left Sicily in 830 A.D., and at Thessalonica embraced the monastic life. Removing later to Constantinople, he entered the monastery of the Studium. There he devoted himself to hymn writing. He was by far the most voluminous writer of hymns of the Greek Church, his verses exceeding in number those of St. Gregory of Nazianzus. There are nearly two hundred canons from his pen in the Menaea, and when we consider that each canon is made up of eight odes, to say nothing of the accompanying contakia, it is easy to gauge the extent of his work in that one class of composition. Like most other voluminous writers, however, his quality is not of the best. Many of the canons are exceedingly poor, and reflect little credit on the writer. "Stars of the morning, so gloriously bright," a cento by Dr. Neale, gives a very good sample of his use of figure. "Far from Thy heavenly care," a contakion after the sixth ode of the canon for Septuagesima, perhaps owes more to the translator than at first sight appears. St. Joseph died, 883.

Theoctistus

Theoctistus was a friend of St. Joseph, and was a monk at the Studium at Constantinople in the latter part of St. Joseph's residence at that famous monastery, about the middle of the ninth century. Very little is known about Theoctistus, and the only hymnodical work which can be attributed to him with certainty, is a very attractive canon in the Parakletike, called The Supplicant Canon of Theoctistus to Jesus. A cento from that canon beginning "Jesus, name all names above," is in common use.

Metrophanes of Smyrna

Metrophanes, Bishop of Smyrna in the latter part of the ninth century, was one of the minor poets of the Greek Church. He composed several canons in honour of the Blessed Trinity, which find a place in the Octoechus. Very little of his work has been translated. Dr. Neale gives a cento from one of the canons in his Hymns of the Eastern Church, which is repeated in The English Hymnal, "O Unity of Threefold Light." Metrophanes died about 910 A.D.

Hymns of the Apostolic Church

INFINITE GOD

tr., John Brownlie
Kurie ho Theos hemon, hou to kratos aneikaston, kai he doxa akataleptos, hou to eleos ametreton, kai he philanthropia aphatos·

I

Our highest thought of God is vain;
Whate'er of knowledge we may know,
Our darkened minds but darker grow,
We ne'er can to the light attain.

II

Beyond the mountain tops that rise,
Still higher altitudes appear;
Climb as we may, we come not near
The peaks that pierce the azure skies.

III

Beyond the farthest stretch of mind,
The wisdom of our God extends;
We touch the love that never ends,
And only know that it is kind.

IV

We cannot gaze upon the sun,
Save through the mists from earth that rise;
God's glory only meets our eyes
When veiled in the Incarnate One.

V

Yea, none but God His love can know,
Nor can The Christ that love express;
The gift is ever something less,
Than is the love the gift would show.

Rev. John Brownlie, D.D.

VI

Our minds, our hearts, our spirits fail
In all our searching God to find;
We only know that He is kind,
And nought that knowledge can assail.

VII

No soul can rise to God, alone,
The height divine we cannot reach;
Do Thou, O Christ, our blindness teach,
Until we know as we are known.

MORNING I
tr., John Brownlie

I

The morning dawns; on gilded height,
The glory of the early light
Awaits the rising sun;
Awake, my soul, to life awake!
Inspired with hope, thy task o'ertake,
And fill the day begun.

II

O Light, beyond our utmost light,
To Whom our day is as the night,
Our sun a feeble star;
Lead me to where Thy glories rise,
Beyond the earth, beyond the skies,
On fairer fields afar.

III

Thou art the Light, Eternal Christ,
Whose glory at the first sufficed
To fire the endless spheres;
Night has no more abiding place,
Before the brightness of Thy face
The darkness disappears.

IV

O that a searching ray might shine
Within this darkened soul of mine,
And bid my night depart!
Then would the joy of life abound,
And summer music ever sound
Within my joyless heart.

Rev. John Brownlie, D.D.

MORNING II
tr., John Brownlie

I

See, from the eastern hills, the morn
Its glowing shafts unsparing flings;
And to a waking world are borne
The light and joy that morning brings:
O God of love, to Thee we raise
Our early song of gladsome praise.

II

There, on the flower-bespangled sod,
The petals open to the sun;
And feathered songsters sing to God,
And hail the cheerful day begun:
With theirs, our early songs unite,
To praise our God Who gives the light.

III

Morn of a better day, we sing
Thy praise, O Christ, Whose wondrous grace
Can brightness to our darkness bring,
And scatter night before Thy face:
Now let our morning praise arise,
A glad accepted sacrifice.

IV

O let our life a morning know,--
The promise of a better day;
And set our night-chilled hearts aglow,
And fill them with Thy joy, we pray:
Then shall our praise to Thee arise,
A glad accepted sacrifice.

Hymns of the Apostolic Church
V

Sun of our life, O Christ, art Thou;
No clouds depress when Thou art near;
Come with Thy radiant beauty now,
And let that morn of joy appear:
Glad shall our songs of praise arise
When morn is shining in our skies.

MORNING III
tr., John Brownlie

I

Light in the dark, before the dawn awaking
Brings in the east the growing light of day,
Comes to the soul that, earthly lights forsaking,
Lives in the light that never dies away.

II

Here, light and dark, and sun, and cloud, and sadness,
Come to the soul that makes the world its all;
There, endless noon, and unabating gladness,
Reign in a realm where night can never fall.

III

Live in my soul, O Light of lights supernal,
Charged with the joy that rising morning gives;
Be Thou my foretaste of the light eternal,
Bright in the realm where joy unfailing lives.

IV

Christ, to my soul, be all my soul-desiring,
Seeks in a land where light and darkness come;
And, when set free, to fairer fields aspiring,
There let me find with Thee a lasting home.

MORNING IV
tr., John Brownlie

I

Awake! the morn is here,
The long, dark night is past;
The gladness and the light appear,
And beauty shines at last.

II

Awake! the morning sings,
The clouds have passed away;
The rising sun triumphant brings
The long-expected day.

III

Awake! the Christ arose
The first faint dawn to greet;
The smiling world in sweetness strews
Its flowers among His feet.

IV

Awake, my soul, awake!
Arise on buoyant wings,
The sordid and the sin forsake,
And mount to better things.

V

Immortal Christ, all hail!
Thy power hath triumphed quite;
Sin can no more our souls assail,
Nor death, nor grave, nor night.

Rev. John Brownlie, D.D.

MORNING V
tr., John Brownlie

I

The crimson blush of morning glows
On towering peaks where clouds repose,
And, lo! the sombre robe of night
Is rent with shafts of golden light.

II

O Light Divine, each opening day
Illume our souls with gladdening ray;
And, as the sun his course pursues,
With growing light our lives diffuse.

III

In childhood's morn, when wondering eyes
Behold the light that fills the skies;
And loins art girt at opening day
Life's myriad voices to obey,

IV

O Light Divine, serene and pure,
Shine on a path of life, secure;
Let joy, like songs the morn that greet,
Make music for the willing feet.

V

When, prompted by the will of God,
A path we tread, before untrod;
And doubts our onward course attend,--
Thy light upon our path extend.

VI

O Light of lights, when day is done,
And night pursues our setting sun,
Be ours to hail that better day,
Whose light Thou art eternally.

MORNING VI
tr., John Brownlie

I

The morn awakes; from eastern hills
The golden light creation fills;
And arrows chase the night that flies
Before the ever-brightening skies.

II

The morn awakes; up, soul of mine,
And, like the morn, in beauty shine;
Strong, as the high-ascending sun,
Thy race of duty boldly run.

III

Night for the weary comes at length;
Morn gives the soul the needed strength;
Light shall thy path encircling, cheer,
And melt each lingering cloud of fear.

IV

O Light of lights, when night descends,
And brooding fear my life attends,
Shew to my soul, that night departs
When morning trims her glowing darts.

V

O Christ, Who art my Better Sun,
Bright shines the day with Thee begun;
No terror can the mind oppress,
Nor cloud th' aspiring soul distress.

VI

To Thee, O glorious Light of light,
Be honour paid when morn is bright;
To Father, and to Spirit blest,
Be glory every day exprest.

Rev. John Brownlie, D.D.

MORNING VII
tr., John Brownlie

I

All glorious, see, the morning breaks;
Awake, my soul, creation wakes:
And, while the purple tints the skies,
Prepare for God thy sacrifice.

II

Thanks to my God, my best of friends,
For all the care His love extends;
For rest, and peace, and waking eyes
To view the light that fills the skies.

III

Let sleep my waking eyes forsake;
From sloth my soul her pinions shake;
And may the light that gladdens all
Illume my task till evening fall.

IV

O Christ, my Morning Star, my Light,
With Thee no dread infects the night;
May darkness ne'er my life appal,
Nor night, at noon-tide, darkly fall.

V

Bring me where morn eternal shines,
And light, unfailing, life entwines;
Where darkness ne'er its clouds unrolls
To charge with dread our fearful souls.

VI

To Thee, O Christ, be endless praise,
O Light of lights, my Light always;
Be aye my morn, forever shine,
And fill my soul with peace divine.

EVENING I
tr., John Brownlie

I

The darkness deepens in the skies,
The light before the shadows flies
And earth forsakes;
My prayer, O Christ, in mercy hear,
Keep Thou my soul from doubt and fear,
Till morn awakes.

II

Light of my life, O Christ, Thou art,
Joy of my soul, my trusting heart
Confides in Thee;
Night cannot hide Thy loving face,
Nor bar the outflow of Thy grace,
O Christ, to me.

III

Darker than night that awful day,
When sin and death in grim array,
The Christ assailed;
Now from the Cross, in light serene,
The radiance of the morn is seen,
Where night prevailed.

IV

Lord, may Thy Cross my night subdue,
My morning deck with crimson hue
And golden light;
And all day long, while work is done,
Outshine the brightness of the sun,
Even at its height.

Rev. John Brownlie, D.D.

V

Now, give the weary calm repose
Till morning light in beauty glows,
And life awakes;
And when we sleep the last long sleep,
Safe through the night Thy servants keep,
Till morning breaks.

EVENING II
tr., John Brownlie
Cathismata of the Resurrection

I

Gone is the glowing orb of day,
The hues of sunset fade away,
And all the world is still;
The starlight sparkles to the sight,
As fall the curtains of the night
On every vale and hill.

II

O God, 'twas night when, all too soon,
The dark eclipsed the light at noon;
And men, convulsed with dread,
The Cross upon the hill descried
On which the God-man groaned and died,
With shame upon His head.

III

And night prevailed with dismal gloom
While, 'prisoned in the awful tomb,
The Christ in stillness lay:
But every night a morn precedes,
And darkness into brightness leads,--
And dawned the glorious day.

IV

O God, in mercy, grant that we
The Resurrection light may see
When death's still night is past;
And to the risen Christ arise,
While morning fills th' eternal skies
With glory that shall last.

Rev. John Brownlie, D.D.

V

Gone is the glowing orb of day,
The hues of sunset fade away,
And dark the night descends;
O God, Thy servants guard, we pray,
Till morn awakes another day,
And till life's journey ends.

EVENING III
tr., John Brownlie

I

O Lord of light, Thy beams display,
And waken joy in every heart;
Bring to our souls the light of day,
And bid our brooding night depart.

II

In Thy fair realm there is no gloom,
The radiant day is never done;
They need no candle to illume,
Nor wait the rising of the sun.

III

No morning ushers in the day,
Nor evening marks its slow decline;
There Thou art sun, and shinest aye,
And all the light and joy are Thine.

IV

Eternal Light, Eternal Day,
No eve obscures, no darkness hides;
But clear the noon-tide shines alway,
For there Thy presence aye abides.

V

Come at this hour, O Light divine,
As daylight fades, and night is nigh,
And in our souls with radiance shine,
As Thou art wont in realms on high.

EVENING IV
tr., John Brownlie

I

The sun has reached his western goal,
And night winds hush the world to rest;
Be still, and worship God, my soul,
Who through the day thy life hath blest.

II

To God thy Maker, thanks accord,
For life, and hope, and every good,
And all the comfort of the Word
Incarnate, for the spirit's food.

III

Ah! night is dark when clouds of guilt
The shrinking soul with fears distress,--
Call on the Christ Whose blood was spilt,
And all thy guiltiness confess.

IV

Then let me rest in calm repose,--
Secure in Him, my rest is sweet;
The fears of night no dread impose,
If I have worshipped at His feet.

V

O Christ, Who art my Light, I pray,
Keep Thou my soul till morning shine;
Then, brighter than the orb of day,
Illume my path with light divine.

ADVENT AND CHRISTMAS I
tr., John Brownlie

I

The longing eyes that sought the light
Are filled with glad amaze,
As, from the depths of brooding night,
The morning meets their gaze;
O weary night! its hours are past,
And morning light hath dawned at last.

II

O Christ, Who in the heart of God,
Eternal, did'st repose;
Whom to proclaim to earth abroad,
The seer and prophet rose;
Now comes to earth, Incarnate Word,
To tell the love of God our Lord.

III

Now hearts respond that, mute before,
In night and silence dwelt,--
Who longed, in worship, to adore
A love they never felt;
For night is gone, and silence rings,
And every heart responsive, sings.

IV

Hail, Christ of God! Anointed One,
From sin's dark night to free;
Thou art the One-begotten Son
Whom ages longed to see;
O weary night, its hours are past,
And morning light hath dawned at last.

Rev. John Brownlie, D.D.

ADVENT AND CHRISTMAS II
tr., John Brownlie
O Despotou philanthropias!

I

O Love supreme, exceeding broad,
Great source of love, the love of God,
Outreaching all we know;
High as the heavens where glories shine,
Far towers that mighty love divine,
And deep as hell below.

II

God looked from heaven on man's estate,
To view our need exceeding great,
And all our loss and shame;
And God Incarnate came to earth,
The Godman by mysterious birth,
And bore our sinful name.

III

He walked the earth, but all unknown;
In vain the love of God was shown,
For sinners spurned His grace;
And while He pled, they mocking cried,
"Away, let Him be crucified,"
And mocked Him to His face.

IV

They raised Him up 'twixt earth and sky,
And left the Godman there to die,
In all His suffering sore;
And ere He died, the prayer was made
That guilt might not on men be laid,
For all the ill He bore.

V

O love supreme, so broad, so high!
Here, prostrate, at the Cross I lie,
But I adore and praise;
For me, for me, Thy blood was spilt,
Mine is the sin, and mine the guilt--
O God, my guilt erase.

Rev. John Brownlie, D.D.

ADVENT AND CHRISTMAS III
tr., John Brownlie
angeloi meta poimenon doxazousi.

I

A band of herdsmen tarried late,
Through hours of night disconsolate;
Around, the snow lay glistening white,
And stars o'erhead were shining bright;
O favoured shepherds, there shall rise
A brighter star in yonder skies.

II

Whence comes this glory, brighter far
Than light that shines from midnight star?
An angel from the Lord appears,
And lo! their minds are filled with fears;
O favoured shepherds, wherefore fear?
The messenger of God is here.

III

"O band of herdsmen, list! I bring
Glad tidings of a promised King;
Go, in a manger ye shall find
The new-born Saviour of mankind;"
O favoured shepherds, such surprise!
To see the Christ in mean disguise.

IV

Then stood the herdsmen all amaze,
For heaven with glory was ablaze;
And choirs of angels, clad in white,
Awoke with song the silent night;
O favoured shepherds, ye were blest,
To hear that heavenly song exprest.

V

To God be glory," thus they sang,
While earth and heaven with music rang;
"And peace abounding henceforth dwell

With those on earth who please me well;"
O favoured shepherds, night is past,
And morn, bright morn, is come at last.

VI

O band of herdsmen, long ago,
That song was sung on earth below,
Now myriad hosts uplift the strains
That first awoke on Bethlehem's plains;
O favoured shepherds, round the throne,
The angel's song is now your own.

Rev. John Brownlie, D.D.

PASSIONTIDE AND EASTER I
tr., John Brownlie
Doxa kurie to Stauro sou.

I

They set the Cross upon a hill,
And led Him forth to die;
And while the wondering heavens were still,
They nailed the Christ on high.

II

And hosts beheld in blank dismay,
The power to sinners given,
To raise their wicked hands to slay
The mighty King of Heaven.

III

O patience of Almighty God!
O love of Christ the Son!
To lie beneath the awful rod,
Until the task was done.

IV

O sin of man! O cruel sin!
Who can its vileness tell?
That slew the Christ Who came to win
The souls He loved so well.

V

Praise to Thy Cross, Immortal Christ!
For Thou didst die to live;
And that the gift of life, unpriced,
Thou mightst to sinners give.

PASSIONTIDE AND EASTER II
tr., John Brownlie
tetelestai!

I

Lo, He is dead! The suffering Christ is dead;
Closed are His eyes, and bowèd is His head.

II

Dead, too, in shame! Upon a Cross! and see,
Thorns crown His brow, in stinging mockery.

III

O night, and woe! The sun and stars are gone;
Dark is the world, and hope, despairing, flown.

IV

Art Thou not Christ? the Son of God, art Thou?
How then this death? This awful silence, how?

V

O sin and death, and victory of the grave!
Canst Thou, in death, O Christ, Thy people save?

VI

Weep in the night, O mortals, at the grave;
Dead is the Christ, and dead He cannot save.

Rev. John Brownlie, D.D.

PASSIONTIDE AND EASTER III
tr., John Brownlie
Christos aneste ek nekron.

I

Morning awakes, and morn awaking sings;
Light speeds from heaven to earth with glowing wings.

II

Haste to the tomb! Ye mourners, haste, with glee!
Christ hath arisen, from death's grim fetters free.

III

Gone are the night, the terror, and the gloom;
Christ hath arisen, and left the awful tomb.

IV

Death now is dead, the grave hath lost its power;
Death and the grave are vanquished at this hour.

V

Thou art the Christ, victorious Christ art Thou,
Death has no sting, and grave no victory now.

VI

Glory to Thee, O Christ, Thy people bring;
Thou art our God, and our Immortal King.

PASSIONTIDE AND EASTER IV
tr., John Brownlie

I

Life from the dead the King Immortal gives,
Who from the grave arose and ever lives;
Slain is the foe, the foe by death is slain,
By Him Who died, and rose to life again.

II

Sight to the blind this morn of beauty brings,
As from the dark it speeds with glowing wings;
Grope they no more, nor stumble in the night;
Christ hath arisen, the one Immortal Light.

III

Joy to the sad, to hearts by sorrow wrung;
Gone are the clouds that dark and threatening hung;
Night weeps no more, for lo! the morn awakes,
And all creation into music breaks.

IV

Hope to the lost, among the wilds forlorn,
Far from their home, by prickly tangle torn;
Straight to the eye the path ascending lies,
Clear in the light that fills the morning skies.

V

Mortals awake! The Resurrection morn,
Fresh from the dark of death's grim night is born;
Mortals awake! the morn in beauty glows;
Life is the gift the risen Lord bestows.

PASSIONTIDE AND EASTER V
tr., John Brownlie

I

Light more glorious than the sun,
Dawns upon our fearful night;
And the longed for day, begun,
Pours its everlasting light;
Christ hath risen, with gladness, then,
Hail His rising, sons of men.

II

Women came at early gloom,
Sad at heart, and full of fears,
Bearing to the dismal tomb
Spices mingled with their tears;
"Wherefore weep?" the angel said,
"Christ hath risen from the dead."

III

Lone disciples, all amazed,
Sought the place where He had lain;
And they knew not as they gazed,
That their Lord had risen again;--
Mortals, hail the day begun,
Christ hath risen, our glorious Sun.

IV

Mourners, lo! the Christ hath risen,--
Lord of Life, and Lord of Light;
Broken now is hades' prison;
Sin is wounded in the fight;
Lo! we hail Thy rising, now,
Christ, the King Immortal, Thou.

PASSIONTIDE AND EASTER VI
tr., John Brownlie
thanato thanaton kathesas.

I

The gate of life stands wide,
For Christ hath entered in;
Now fearless mount the upward path,
Nor dread the power of sin;
For sin and death were slain
By Him Who rose again.

II

'Twas on the Cross He died,
And death a victory won,
Short lived as night that flies before
The rising of the sun;--
For death by Christ was slain
Who died to live again.

III

The might of sin prevailed,--
Its cruel hate and scorn,--
It drove the cruel spear and nails,
And crowned the Christ with thorn;
The spear was broke in twain
By Christ Who rose again.

IV

Up, mortals! life is yours,
The prize is yours to win;
For Christ hath vanquished by His might,
The power of death and sin;
For sin and death were slain
By Christ Who rose again.

Rev. John Brownlie, D.D.

V

To thee, O Christ, be praise,
Whose power decayeth never;
To Father, and to Holy Ghost,
Be laud, and glory, ever;
For death by Christ was slain,
Who died to live again.

PASSIONTIDE AND EASTER VII
tr., John Brownlie

I

Go, tell the world the Lord hath risen,
See, empty stands the mortal prison;
Now morn illumes the eastern skies,
Awake my soul! with Christ arise.

II

Dawn of a day no night shall shroud,
When sun declines in darkling cloud;
But brighter still, and brighter glows,
As morn illumes and noontide glows.

III

Go, tell the world that death no more
Rules with the power he held before;
For, in the grave, the Lord of life
The tyrant crushed in glorious strife.

IV

Why bear ye spices for the dead?
Lo! He is risen, even as He said,
And empty stands the mortal prison,--
Go, tell the world that Christ hath risen.

V

Glory to Thee, O Christ our King,
Our hearts, our songs, our voices bring;
For sin is crushed, and death is slain,
By Him Who died and rose again.

Rev. John Brownlie, D.D.

PASSIONTIDE AND EASTER VIII
tr., John Brownlie

I

The stone is rolled away,
The Christ hath left the tomb;
Come, see the place where once He lay,
Amid its awful gloom;
And bring no spices for the dead,
For He is risen, even as He said.

II

Awake! the morn is here;
Awake! the night is o'er;
And lo! the shadows disappear,
To visit earth no more;
The sun that wakes our glorious day
Shall shine upon the world for aye.

III

Hence now the Cross and woe;
Hence now the cruel spite;
The weary wanderings here below,
The death, the grave, the night;
The power of sin is thrust aside,
The gates of life are opened wide.

IV

Now sin and death are slain;
The grave and hades groan;
For He Who died now lives again,
The triumph is His own;
No thorns afflict His aching brow,
He wears the Victor's garland now.

Hymns of the Apostolic Church
V

Hail! risen Christ, our God,
The world rejoicing sings;
Proclaim the tidings far abroad,
That Christ is King of kings;
A King by right of conquest, He
Sits on His throne of majesty.

Rev. John Brownlie, D.D.

PASSIONTIDE AND EASTER IX
tr., John Brownlie

I

Glory to God, the promised day awakes,
And light eternal on our darkness breaks.

II

Hail to the King, the King that comes to reign;
Burst are our bands, and we are free again.

III

He Who in shame the Cross of anguish bore,
Now lives to reign in glory evermore.

IV

Death and the grave, and sin, have lost their sway;
Death is destroyed, and sin is borne away.

V

Hades' abode that lay in silent night,
Hailed with acclaim the dawning of the light.

VI

Hail to the Christ, Who mounts His throne again;
Life is His gift unto the sons of men.

VII

Thou art the Christ, Eternal Christ art Thou;
We rise with Thee to life immortal now.

PASSIONTIDE AND EASTER X
tr., John Brownlie

I

Light, ere the dawn in beauty broke,
Sprang from the darkness and the gloom,
When Christ the King from death awoke,
And burst the fetters of the tomb.

II

Light of our souls! a glorious day
Broke on the darkness of our world;
Hell and his hosts, in black array,
From their usurpèd power were hurled.

III

Hope of the hearts with anguish wrung,
Light of the eyes bedimmed by woe,--
When, on the Cross forsaken, hung,
He Who had shared their life below.

IV

All hail, the Christ! Immortal, Thou!
Death and the grave are conquered quite;
Gone is the power that held us, now,
Gone are the terrors of the night.

Rev. John Brownlie, D.D.

PASSIONTIDE AND EASTER XI
tr., John Brownlie
epi tes theias phulakes.

I

Watchman, from the height beholding,
Look towards the eastern sky;
Is the light of heaven unfolding?
Comes the radiant angel nigh,
Telling to our lost creation
Christ hath risen for our salvation?

II

Yea, He came to earth to save us,--
As a lamb, the Christ was slain;
For our Passover He gave us
His own flesh, in direst pain;
On a Cross of anguish dying,
Very God, our need supplying.

III

Watchman, from the height beholding,
Comes the angel through the gloom,
Ere the morning light unfolding
Fills the darkness of the tomb?
Comes the angel through the sadness,
Waking souls of men to gladness?

IV

See the gates of hades shaken;
Burst asunder is the prison;
Souls of men from bondage taken,
Praise the Lord, from death arisen;
Hail the Resurrection morning,
All our life with hope adorning.

PASSIONTIDE AND EASTER XII
tr., John Brownlie

I

At earliest dawn the Lord awoke,
True Light upon our dismal gloom,
And from the darkness of the tomb
Arose ere yet the morning broke.

II

Vainly the watchers lingered nigh:
No watch could stay immortal power,
Nor stone nor seal at that great hour,
The heavenly messenger defy.

III

Like flax before the living flame,
The bands of death asunder break,
And ere the sons of men awake,
The Christ from death's grim shadows came.

IV

Morning awake! a Morn is here;
Welcome its dawn on darker night,
Than flies before the rising light
When tinged with gold thy beams appear.

V

Morning awake! the night shall fall,
And quench the light thy rising gives;
The Light Immortal ever lives,
True Light that comes to lighten all.

VI

Glory to Thee, O Christ, we bring--
Glad from the tomb Thy Light we greet,
Thy rising hail with praises meet,
O Thou Immortal Christ our King.

Rev. John Brownlie, D.D.

PASSIONTIDE AND EASTER XIII
tr., John Brownlie
ge de agalliastho· Christos gar egegertai.

I

Sleepers awake! the night's long reign is past;
Purple and gold adorn the hills at last;
Songs of delight from myriad hearts arise,
Borne on the wind that bears them to the skies.

II

Sleepers awake! The Christ from death awakes;
Light from the tomb in radiant beauty breaks;
Song from the heavens to listening earth descends;
Gladness of earth with heavenly gladness blends.

III

Sleepers awake! to hope immortal spring,
Mount to the heights with never tiring wing;
Clouds are of earth where linger doubt and fear,
There, in the light, no threatening clouds appear.

IV

Sleepers awake! no time for slumber now,
Day shines from heaven with glory on its brow.
Darkness and night, and clouds are passed away,
Christ is the Light of our Eternal Day.

V

Sleepers awake! the night's long reign is past;
Purple and gold adorn the hills at last;
Christ hath arisen, awake! creation wakes,
Light everlasting on our darkness breaks.

PASSIONTIDE AND EASTER XIV
tr., John Brownlie
Christos aneste ek nekron, thanato thanaton patesas.

I

What wonder wakes a sleeping world,
And gives the morn her crown?
Death from usurped dominion hurled,
By death is trodden down.

II

And slaves in fettered bondage cast,
Their glorious Victor hail,
For lo! the reign of death is past,
The grave and hades quail.

III

And night is gone, and morn is here,
And clouds no longer frown;
For death that filled the soul with fear,
By death is trodden down.

IV

O Christ, Immortal from the tomb!
To Thee our songs arise--
Thou, Who hast filled our dismal gloom
With light of Paradise.

V

And Thou shalt wear a glorious crown,
Who wore the crown of thorns,
Since death by death is trodden down,
This glorious Morn of morns.

VI

Let earth and sky, and all who dwell
In hades' dark abode,
With cheerful voice the chorus swell,
Of praise to Christ our God.

Rev. John Brownlie, D.D.

VII

Awake, my soul! to praise arise,
And give The Christ His crown,
Who mounts Immortal to the skies--
For death is trodden down.

PASSIONTIDE AND EASTER XV
tr., John Brownlie
hos egerthe ho kurios, thanatosas ton thanaton.

I

Glorious from the field of strife,
Lo! the Victor mounts His throne;
Lord of death and King of life,
His the triumph, His alone--
Glorious from the field of strife,
Christ, Immortal King of Life.

II

Wake to gladness, sons of men!
Heaven, your gates eternal raise!
Welcome to your bliss again
Him, the worthiest of praise,--
Glorious from the field of strife,
Christ, Immortal King of Life.

III

Ah! the rage of angry foes,
Ah! the garments rolled in blood;
Where were dealt the fiercest blows,
There the valiant Victor stood--
Glorious on the field of strife,
Christ, Immortal King of Life.

IV

Sin and death--the twain assailed,
And the Christ expiring fell;
But the Death o'er death prevailed,
And the might of sin and hell;
Victor from the field of strife,
Hail! Immortal King of Life.

Rev. John Brownlie, D.D.

PASSIONTIDE AND EASTER XVI
tr., John Brownlie

I

The light that from the fire of love
With glory girds the throne above,
Falls on our world by sin undone,
All radiant as the morning sun.

II

O souls of men, in darkness lost,
Look upwards where the shining host,
Like stars around the Christ are set,
More bright than earthly coronet.

III

These are the souls of men restored,
By Him Whose blood on earth was poured,
Who, though a Son, was bound and led
To where His heart in anguish bled.

IV

Death at the Christ in fury sprung,
As on the Cross He meekly hung;
But by His dying, death was slain,
And sin, and all their hideous train.

V

O souls of men, to such a prize,
Thine is the power with these to rise;
No barrier flung across the way
Can stay thy course to endless day.

VI

O deathless Christ! O sinless One!
Son of the Father, God's own Son,
Thine is the power from sin to free
Their souls who put their trust in Thee.

Hymns of the Apostolic Church
VII

Glory to Thee, O Christ, be given
By souls redeemed in earth and heaven;
Our souls, exulting, seek the place
Where dwells the fulness of Thy grace.

Rev. John Brownlie, D.D.

PASSIONTIDE AND EASTER XVII
tr., John Brownlie
Kurie, e en pollais hamartias.

    This Idiomelon, the original of which may be seen at p. 384 of the Athens edition of the Triodion, bears the title, poiema Kassiannes Monaches ("A poem of Kassia the Recluse"). It is still sung on Wednesday of Holy Week.

    Kassia had been chosen as consort by the Emperor Theophilos the Iconoclast (A.D. 829-843), son of Michael II. the Stammerer, and when she was brought into his presence, the Emperor greeted her, exclaiming, "Woman is the source of all evil;" to which Kassia replied, "And also of all good." Trifling as the circumstance may seem, it roused the anger of the monarch, and the match was broken off.

    Thereupon Kassia devoted herself to religion, and founded a nunnery, in which she remained till her death. In the quiet and seclusion of her life, she wrote many idiomela, which are scattered over the Greek Office Books, chiefly The Menaea.

    None of her poetry, so far as the present writer has been able to discover, has ever been rendered into English. Certainly this, which is one of the finest of her idiomela, appears here for the first time in English verse. It is brimful of pathos and tinged with melancholy, without doubt traceable to the sad experiences of her life. May it not be that in the second line of the first stanza there is a suggestion of her own name? k?sia (kasia) is sometimes written kassia (kassia), the sweet herb. The sweetness of cassia had been changed to the bitterness of myrrh.

I

Burdened with sin, more, Lord, than I can tell,
I bear the myrrh with those that loved Thee well;
And to the grave lamenting, lo, I bring,
For this last solemn rite, my offering.

II

The love of sin, ah, that it should be so,
That held my truant spirit long ago,--
That love of sin my foolish heart hath found,
And moonless night now circles me around.

III

O Thou, Who by the clouds that drape the sky,
Bearest the waters of the sea on high,
Accept the offering of my bitter tears,

From springs that issue in a night of fears.

IV

O Thou, Who mad'st the heavens of old to bow,
Incline Thine ear and hear Thy servant now,
And let my sighing and my grievous moan,
Enter Thine ear, O God, my God alone.

V

Prostrate I fall, and in my worship meet,
Would kiss amid my tears Thy stainless feet,
And wipe them with my hair, that by Thy grace,
I with the penitent may take my place.

VI

To Thy fair Paradise, when eve has come,
Take Thou Thy servant in Thy mercy home;
From fear of Judgment, and from evil free,
There let me dwell for evermore with Thee.

Rev. John Brownlie, D.D.

ASCENSION I
tr., John Brownlie
kai ten pros hupsos ouranou theian analepsin.

I

He mounts to where the azure shines,
Triumphant as the light;
Till, past the glowing gates, The Christ
Is lost to mortal sight.

II

And now amid the bliss of heaven,
The Father's throne He shares;
And gems of radiant beauty deck
The sparkling crown He wears.

III

Remember, Lord, Thy promise made,
When hearts in sadness pined,
And send the Comforter to soothe
The sorrows of mankind;

IV

And as the lingering ages pass,
To teach the souls of men,
That they may hail the Christ when He
In glory comes again.

V

All praise to Thee, Eternal God,
And to the Son be given,
Whose glory, darkly veiled on earth,
Now fills the light of heaven;

VI

And to the Holy Comforter,
By Whom our lives are blest,
Be praise, by every waiting heart,
For evermore expressed.

ASCENSION II
tr., John Brownlie

I

See the King of kings ascending
To His throne of power again;
Who in humble garb descending,
Came to dwell with lowly men.

II

Glad the angel hosts adoring
Fling the golden gates aside;
Mortals, view the Victor soaring,
Heaven receives the Lord with pride.

III

Strike your harps, ye choirs supernal;
Lift your songs of welcome now;
For, behold your King eternal
Comes with laurels on His brow.

IV

Gone the sorrow and the sighing;
All the anguish and the pain;
Gone the weakness and the dying,--
Choirs immortal, raise the strain;

V

Hallelujah! endless glory
To the King of Glory give;
Mortals, heed the gladsome story,
Christ is risen, and thou may'st live.

Rev. John Brownlie, D.D.

ASCENSION III
tr., John Brownlie

I

Now let the gates be lifted up,
That Christ may enter in,
Who drank for man the bitter cup,
And crushed the power of sin;
He enters, lo! a Victor brave,
Triumphant from the yawning grave.

II

Did death and hell their power unite
To hold their prize? in vain;
For morn awoke upon the night,
And death and hell were slain;
All hail the Victor from the grave,
Who rose from death our souls to save.

III

Now let the Christ His right assume,--
The throne of high renown;
No more do thorns His temples fret,
He wears a regal crown;--
Up, myriad hosts, your praises bring,
And laud the All-victorious King.

IV

To God the Father, God the Son,
And God the Spirit blest,
Be glory while the ages run,
By angel hosts exprest;
And souls from death's dark bondage won,
By Christ, the All-victorious Son.

ASCENSION IV
tr., John Brownlie

I

Wrapt in wonder and amaze,
On the throne of God I gaze;--
Sparkling are the gems abounding,
Sweet the harps and viols sounding;
See the palms of victory wave,--
'Twas the Christ the triumph gave.

II

Lo, He sits in glory now,
Thorns no longer clutch his brow,--
Glory, laud, and honour bringing,
Choirs of the redeemed are singing,--
Thus the King enthroned they greet,
And their crowns are at His feet.

III

Past, the life He lived below,
Gone the weariness and woe;
Now the painful strife is ended,
Christ a victor hath ascended,
Sin and death are bound with chains,
And the King Immortal reigns.

IV

Ah! Good Lord, when life is past,
Bring me to such bliss at last;
Where love wakens gleams of gladness,
In the eyes that wept for sadness;--
Where the weary rest, and praise
Christ, the Victor King, always.

Rev. John Brownlie, D.D.

ASCENSION V
tr., John Brownlie
anephereto eis ton ouranon.

I

A Love divine, exceeding broad,
Shines glorious from the throne of God,
Where Christ above all power is set,
Who rose to reign from Olivet.

II

A mercy great to sinners brought,
Exceeding far man's kindest thought,
Wide as the hope to mortals given,
Springs from that love enthroned in heaven.

III

Far as the need of man extends,
The grace of Christ our life attends;
For love enthroned can ne'er forget
The tears and joys of Olivet.

IV

And mercy still the love obeys
That ever loved, and loves always,
And from the bliss of heaven descends
To seek the soul that love befriends.

V

O King of Life, Immortal One!
Thy grace extend to souls undone,
Nor on the throne of heaven forget
The tears and joys of Olivet.

PENTECOST I
tr., John Brownlie

I

When Jesus at the feast reclined,
And sad disciples sorrowed most,
He gave, to soothe their troubled mind,
The promise of the Holy Ghost.

II

"I will not leave you," thus He spake,
"As orphans here alone to dwell;
With you My sure abode I'll make,
And all your loneliness dispel."

III

And when amid the clouds of heaven,
Th' ascending Lord to sight was lost;
The promised Gift of Christ was given
Upon the hallowed Pentecost.

IV

He came upon a rushing wind,
The faint apostles to inspire;
And on their waiting band declined,
In form of cloven tongues of fire.

V

And as the Spirit utterance gave,
Their tongues expressed the thought inspired;
And faltering, timid hearts were brave,
And fainting souls with zeal were fired.

VI

O Spirit, Gift of Christ adored,
Our need behold, in power descend;
And, as was promised by our Lord,
Abide our Comforter, and Friend.

PENTECOST II
tr., John Brownlie
zoes choregos, elthe, kai skenoson en hemin, kai katharison hemas apo pases kelidos.

I

O Spirit, Lord Almighty, Blest,
Of all the Gifts of Christ the Best;
Come with Thy power, our lives control,
The weak make strong, the sin-sick whole.

II

Let Thy pervading light reveal
The sin our subtle hearts conceal;
And when we humbly guilt confess,
Let penitence our souls possess.

III

O Spirit, God of love and light,
Shine on the Cross in sin's dark night,
And there reveal the Christ of God,
Bruised for our sin beneath the rod.

IV

Shine on the road that upward tends,
Where Christ the pilgrim soul befriends;
Where 'mid the toil our spirit feels,
The promised aid Thy grace reveals.

V

O Spirit, Lord of love and power,
Help Thou the soul in needful hour;
Thy soothing balm in love bestow,
Through all our troubled life below.

Hymns of the Apostolic Church
VI

Glory to Thee, the Risen Christ,
Through Whom the gift of love unpriced,
From God the source of every good,
Descends to us in plenitude.

PENTECOST III
tr., John Brownlie

I

O Holy Ghost, eternal Lord,
One with the Father and the Word;
Who art, and wast, and aye shalt be,
While ages pass, eternally.

II

Thou spring of Life, Thou source of Light,
Fountain of Goodness, God of Might;
By Thee the Love of God is known,
And Christ in all His fulness shown.

III

O Lord of grace, how good Thou art,
To soothe with balm the wounded heart;
To fire with zeal the fainting soul,
To teach, to comfort, and control.

IV

To Thee eternal praise be given,
Thou Light of earth, Thou Joy of heaven;
Who from the Immortal Father came,
In living tongues of fiery flame.

V

Eternal Spirit, One in Three--
Father and Son unite with Thee,
In one great, glorious Trinity,
Now, and for evermore to be. Amen.

PENTECOST IV
tr., John Brownlie

I

Eternal Spirit, Lord of grace,
Descend, and in each waiting heart,
Find a preparéd resting-place,
And all Thy sevenfold gifts impart.

II

Our sins reveal, our awful blame,
Shew in the light Thy truth supplies;
And as we feel our guilty shame,
Lead to the Cross where Jesus dies.

III

To needy souls give rich supplies;
Let comfort calm the troubled mind;
Give seeing to the sightless eyes;
Heal all the sorrows of mankind.

IV

Where doubts becloud, or fears distress,
Thy peace her healing balm apply;
Thy light, the night clouds that oppress,
Chase from our dark and threatening sky.

V

Our languid souls that lifeless live,
Revive anew, O Heavenly Breath;
The Holy inspiration give,
That saves the drooping soul from death.

Rev. John Brownlie, D.D.

PENTECOST V
tr., John Brownlie

I

O God of grace, Thou Spirit blest,
Find in our hearts a place to rest,
And there abide for aye;
And let Thy soothing comfort heal
The smarting wounds our spirits feel,
And all our fears allay.

II

When, of the dismal past, misspent,
Our stricken souls in grief repent
And shun the memory drear;
Then, let Thy sweet forgiving grace,
Reveal to us the Father's face,
And scatter all our fear.

III

When, fearful, to the hidden goal,
With timid flight the anxious soul
Would upward, onward press;
Rend Thou the brooding clouds of fear,
To let the cheering light appear,
The doubting soul to bless.

IV

O God of comfort, Spirit blest,
Find in our hearts a place to rest,
And give a calm, secure;--
The past of all its threatening shorn,
The future shining like the morn,
With light that shall endure.

JUDGMENT I
tr., John Brownlie

I

O Lord of mercy, at Thy gate
I loudly knock though coming late,
And seek to enter in;
Noon passed with all its promise clear,
The day declined, now night is here--
Forgive, O Lord, my sin.

II

I wandered while the daylight shone,
Nor thought until the light had flown
How far my feet had strayed;
I said, "My wanderings I'll control,"
But while the world sang to my soul,
I sinfully delayed.

III

O let me in--I see the light,
Its golden arrows pierce the night,
But all without is drear,
And cold, and chill; O night winds, bear
The burden of my heart-born prayer,
And bring it to His ear.

IV

I hear the music and the song,
The laughter of the gleeful throng
That fill the festal hall;
The night dews fall, I've journeyed far--
O wilt Thou not the gate unbar,
In answer to my call?

V

Thou sought'st, O Lord, the wandering child,
By wood and stream, and moorland wild,
When Thou on earth did'st dwell;
The fold, secure, was left behind,

Rev. John Brownlie, D.D.

That Thou might'st seek the lost, and find
Whom Thou did'st love so well.

VI

Yea, 'tis Thy voice! the gate unbar,--
O let me in, I've travelled far,
The midnight wind is chill;
O Christ, what means the silent dread?
Why is the voice of gladness dead,
And all within so still?

VII

Yea, 'tis His voice--Thy servant hears,
Speak, Lord! "Depart?" O night, and fears!
O deepest, darkest woe!
"Depart, for thou hast come too late,
The day is gone, and closed the gate,
Hence from My presence go!"

JUDGMENT II
tr., John Brownlie

I

When God for judgment sets His throne,
And man to wrath awakes;
When rending rocks from heights are cast,
And earth's foundation shakes;
What then, my soul, shall be thy plea,
When God to Judgment summons thee?

II

When, as a garment waxen old,
The heavens are rolled away;
And as a vesture changed for that
Which shall endure for aye,--
How clad, my soul, wilt thou appear,
When God to Judgment draweth near?

III

When loud and shrill the trumpet's blare,
Shall wake the earth and sea;
And from the hidden depths shall rise
The bondman and the free,--
Where, then, my soul, wilt thou abide,
When God at Judgment shall preside?

IV

When from the Record men shall hear
The Judge of all recite;
And every hidden work behold,
Made manifest in light,--
Wilt thou, my soul, the Judgment bear,
That finds the sinner everywhere?

Rev. John Brownlie, D.D.

V

O Christ, Thou Judge, on that dread day,
When sinners shun thy face,
Join not my soul with wicked men,
But free me by Thy grace;
And to my favoured soul be given,
Thy welcome to the bliss of heaven.

JUDGMENT III
tr., John Brownlie

I

Watchers, let your lights be burning,
Soon the Bridegroom will be here;
List! the footsteps now returning,
Rise to greet Him, He is near;
See your lights are trimmed and burning,
For your Lord at His returning.

II

Wake, awake, no time for sleeping,
Though the midnight hour be dark;
Faithfully your vigil keeping,
You shall greet Him;--watchers, hark!
Footsteps tell your Lord's returning,
See your lights are trimmed and burning.

III

Ah, the shame when He appeareth,--
Sleeping watchers, flickering light;
Ah, the sorrow when He neareth,
In the middle of the night;--
Drowsy, in the dark reclining,
While a myriad lights are shining.

IV

Ah, my soul, bestir thee, wake thee,
Day is passing, soon 'tis night;
If the midnight hour o'ertake thee,
Will thy lamp send forth its light?
Wake, awake, thy Lord returneth,
See your light is trimmed and burneth.

JUDGMENT IV
tr., John Brownlie

I

When the Lord to earth returning,
Meets His followers in the air,
With desire within you burning,
Wilt thou mount to greet Him there?
Ah, the transport of the meeting!
Souls of men their Saviour greeting.

II

Watch, the days are quickly flying,
Keep your garments clean and white;
Life grows old, and time is dying,
And His throne is girt with light,
To His searching eye revealing
Stains the dark is now concealing.

III

Do the task your hand is finding;
Bear the burden wisely given;
For the fight your buckler binding,
Seek the aid of highest heaven;--
Doing, bearing, fighting, praying,
Thus the will of God obeying.

IV

When the Lord to earth returning,
Meets the faithful by and by,
Souls with holy ardour burning
Who can mount, shall seek the sky;--
Ah, the transport of the meeting,
Souls of men their Saviour greeting.

VICTORY I
tr., John Brownlie

I

Behold the victor host appear,
With laurels won in mortal strife;
Undaunted by the threat of fears,
When marshalled by the Prince of Life.

II

The Prince upon His throne awaits,
As, forward, upward like a tide,
They win the everlasting gates,
Thrust by angelic hosts aside.

III

Glory to Christ, their song proclaims,
And heart and voice give worship meet;
While, as they shout their loud acclaims,
They lay their laurels at His feet.

IV

O victor hosts who strive no more,
May we, inspired, the fight maintain;
That when our strife with sin is o'er,
We may with you like bliss attain.

V

O Christ our Lord, to Thee we sing;
Thy grace extend till life is past;
And we our crowns exulting bring,
To lay them at Thy feet at last.

Rev. John Brownlie, D.D.

VICTORY II
tr., John Brownlie

I

The saints of God in yonder realm,
Have crowns of varied gem;
Outshining far in brilliant sheen,
Earth's fairest diadem;
And they whose brows are decked with light,
Are crowned as victors in the fight.

II

The palms they wear in yonder realm,
And wave before the throne,
Proclaim the triumph they achieved,
When sin was overthrown;--
Those palms were won where willows grow,
Beside the weeping streams below.

III

The robes of white in yonder realm,
All glistening as the snow,
Were washed in streams that from the Cross
Of bitter anguish flow;
No filthy stain their whiteness mars,
They shine in beauty as the stars.

IV

The praise they sing in yonder realm,--
The songs from lips that rise,
Were tuned in night where hearts are sad,
And sorrow fills the eyes;
The weeping songs that 'woke the night,
Now thrill the land of fadeless light.

V

O Jesus Christ, to yonder realm,
Thy longing children bring;
And give them crowns, and palms, and robes,
And songs of praise, to sing;
And grant them here, by grace to win,
In conflict with the powers of sin.

Rev. John Brownlie, D.D.

VICTORY III
tr., John Brownlie
Martures Christou.

I

The saints of God who sufferings bore,
Who in the strife were steadfast proved,
Now wear in light for evermore,
The crowns conferred by Him they loved.

II

Ten thousand thousand, passing ken,
Their numbers who surround the throne;
Best of the valiant sons of men,
Who scorned their Master to disown.

III

They pledged their fealty to His cause,
And bore the brunt of many a fight;
Nor sought for gain nor vain applause,
But aye were loyal to the right.

IV

Alone they stood in evil day,
While others let the standard fall;
Or bravely trod the upward way,
Obedient to the heavenly call.

V

High in the heavens behold them stand;
Theirs is the joy the saints secure,--
A welcome to their Lord's right hand,
A kingdom that shall aye endure.

VI

Angelic hosts triumphant sing!
Their deeds relate who fought and won;
And in the army of the King,
Upheld the standard of His Son.

VICTORY IV
tr., John Brownlie

I

The chariots of the Lord are strong,
Their number passeth ken;
Mount them and fight against the wrong,
Ye who are valiant men.

II

Where unabashed, the power of sin
Vaunts an unhindered sway,
Ride, in the strength of God, and win
Fresh laurels in the fray.

III

For freedom wield the sword of might,
And cut the bands that bind;
Strike boldly in the cause of right,
And still fresh laurels find.

IV

Where hands are weak, and hearts are faint,
Through conflict sharp and sore;--
Where hearts that murmur no complaint,
Shrink at the thought of more:

V

There let the power of God be shown,
To quell satanic might;
To rescue those who strive alone,
Despondent in the fight.

VI

Ride on, the chariots of the Lord,
Dispel the hosts of sin;
Ye who are valiant, wield the sword,
And still fresh laurels win.

MEDITATIONS I
tr., John Brownlie

I

Night and a storm, and hearts with sore affright,
Quail in their fears before the tempest's might.

II

Blindly the waves with crested summits roll;
The thunders crash, and terrify the soul.

III

Calmly he sleeps; O Christ, art Thou not Lord?
Speak to the winds, and let them hear Thy word.

IV

Thou hast a power to quell the surging sea,
The waters know Thy voice at Galilee.

V

Wake from Thy sleep! How can the Master sleep,
While danger threatens from the frenzied deep?

VI

Tempest and strife, and angry waves are still;
The waters hear Thy voice, and do Thy will.

VII

Lord of our life, wake to our help we pray,
And still the storms that compass our life's way.

MEDITATIONS II
tr., John Brownlie

I

Darkly the tempest swept,
Over the sea;
Fiercely the billows leapt,
Bounding and free;
Sternly each rower bent,
While in the firmament
Clouds were by lightnings rent,
O'er Galilee.

II

Pillowed, the Master lay,
Rocked by the deep;
Worn with the toil of day,
Weary, asleep;
"Master," they fearful cry,
"Wake to the danger nigh,--
Winds from the threatening sky,
Billows that leap."

III

Calmly the Master rose,--
Winds are assuaged;
Sank into calm repose
Waters that raged;
"Peace!" O Thou Lord of might,
Speak in our dread affright,
When through our troubled night,
Battles are waged.

Rev. John Brownlie, D.D.

MEDITATIONS III
tr., John Brownlie

I

Lord, give me sight for I am blind,
Thy blessed face I cannot see;
But Thou art merciful and kind,--
O let Thy mercy come to me.

II

And hear my prayer amid the cries,
Of surging crowds that round Thee press;
Come near and touch my sealèd eyes,
And let me know Thy power to bless.

III

Didst Thou not come a Light to men,
To fill with light the darkened soul,
To raise the dead to life again,
And make the sin-sick spirit whole?

IV

O touch mine eyes, and let the light
That shines from heaven my spirit find;
I grope, and stumble in the night,
I follow, but am left behind.

V

O Jesus, Lord of heavenly light,
Come to our help, our spirits fill;
And quicken now our inward sight,
That we may know, and do Thy will;

VI

And follow where the path is clear,
Nor linger where the danger lies;
And in the darkness feel no fear,
Because we see Thee with our eyes.

MEDITATIONS IV
tr., John Brownlie

I

O praise the wisdom of our God,
And all His matchless love extol;
Who by the anguish of His rod,
Gives healing to the wounded soul.

II

He brought me low because of sin,
And laid His hand upon me sore;
That I might seek by grace to win,
His power to save from sinning more.

III

He brought me low because His love
Was truer than my kindest thought;
For He would lift me far above
The vanities my soul had sought.

IV

And in the darkness I beheld
A light my eyes had never seen;
And all the strife of sin was quelled,
That came my soul and peace between.

V

'Tis good to sink beneath the rod,
And taste the bitterness of sin,
If thus the matchless love of God,
An entrance to the heart may win.

VI

O Jesus Christ, to Thee be praise,
For Thou wert wounded on the tree;--
O may Thy Cross my spirit raise,
And lift me ever nearer Thee.

Rev. John Brownlie, D.D.

MEDITATIONS V
tr., John Brownlie

I

He climbed the slopes of Olivet
When came the hour of prayer,
And in the stillness, Christ with God
Held close communion there.

II

Then all the noise of life was still,
And all the tongues that fret;
And peace His troubled heart possessed,
Which waiting spirits get.

III

Then sank life's tumult like the waves
On Galilee that frowned;
And in the depth of love divine,
The hate of man was drowned.

IV

Lord, when my soul by carking care,
Has lost its needful rest,
Lead me to where the voice is heard
That comforts the distressed.

V

That even now, in distant days,
My longing soul may get
The rich supplies of grace divine,
That hallowed Olivet.

MEDITATIONS VI
tr., John Brownlie

I

"Thou art my portion," saith my soul,
And I am rich in Thee;
My God, there is no want I crave,
But Thou suppliest to me.

II

The labour of my hands may fail,
My path be girt with care;
But plenty crowns the heavenly board,
And I am welcome there.

III

Like mountain brooks in summer time,
Earth's streams of bliss may fail;
But joys perennial flow from Thee,
When parching droughts prevail.

IV

O, rich and full from God's right hand,
Are joys eternal given;
That stream of bliss can never fail
That has its source in heaven.

V

"Thou art my portion," saith my soul,
I have no want denied,
For from the bounties of Thy grace
Are all my needs supplied.

Rev. John Brownlie, D.D.

MEDITATIONS VII
tr., John Brownlie

I

My soul doth wait on God,
From Him my help proceeds;
His mercy is exceeding broad,
To overtake my needs.

II

He gives His pardoning grace,
When I my sin confess;
Nor ever hides from me His face
In my distressfulness.

III

The Spirit of all power,
Most freely He bestows;
And I am strong in evil hour,
When pressed by direst foes.

IV

O, He has gifts in store,
More rich than wealth commands;
And when His pity I implore,
He fills my empty hands.

V

God, Thou art good and kind,
And full of tender grace;
Have me forever in Thy mind,
Nor hide from me Thy face.

MEDITATIONS VIII
tr., John Brownlie

I

The burden of my sin was great,
My soul with pain was crushed;
And every voice of promise sweet,
Was for the moment hushed.

II

Dark clouds come rolling o'er my head,
And quick the night came down;--
O Christ, if Thine was pain like this,
Thorns were a fitting crown.

III

O night without, and night within,
And doubt, and fear, and dread;
And all my folly and my sin,
Before my eyes were spread.

IV

And not a hand to still my pain,
And not a voice to bless;--
O Christ, did all Thy pain and woe
Give anguish like to this?

V

A morning comes when night is past,
A calm when storms are spent;
And healing to my wounded soul,
My God in mercy sent.

VI

I saw the Cross upon the hill,
I felt the dark come down;--
The anguish of His wounded soul,
The stinging of the crown.

Rev. John Brownlie, D.D.

VII

And as I looked, the morning grew,
The calm of morn was mine;
For ah! the anguish that He bore,
My troubled soul, was thine.

MEDITATIONS IX
tr., John Brownlie

I

Bowed with grief and anguish low,
Weary with the clouded way;
Soul of mine, to Christ I'll go,
All my grief before Him lay:
Tell Him, 'neath the willow shade,
Ah! too long my stay is made.

II

Is there joy by Babel's streams,--
Mute the harp on willow hung,
Ne'er a sunglint or a beam,
Heart, as well as harp unstrung?
Soul of mine, awake! arise!
Seek the sunland and the skies.

III

There the palms in triumph wave,
And the stream life giving flows;
Up, my soul, be strong, be brave,
After night the morning glows,
For the willow's weeping shade
Marks the place where vows are made.

IV

Sprigs of willow, leaves of palm,
Days of grief, and hours of song;
Nights of storm and morning calm,
Come alternate all life long;
Soul of mine, the shade of woe
Leads to where the palm leaves grow.

V

Lead me, O Thou Christ of God,
Where the willows weeping sigh;
Safe the way that Thou hast trod,
E'en with dangers lurking nigh,--

Rev. John Brownlie, D.D.

Past the willows and the grave,
To the land where palm trees wave.

VI

Willows by earth's waters weep,
Palm trees wave beneath its sun;
Christ, my wandering footsteps keep,
Till my pilgrimage is done,
Where no willow marks a grave,
And the palms triumphant wave.

MEDITATIONS X
tr., John Brownlie

I

To praise is comely, O my soul,
To God this homage pay;
The bounty of His grace extol,
In grateful song alway;--
My God; to Thee my praise I bring,
For Thou hast taught my soul to sing.

II

O God, unerring wisdom, Thou,
Unfailing love is Thine;
Teach me to trust that wisdom now,
And on that love recline;--
My God, to Thee my praise I bring,
For Thou hast taught my soul to sing.

III

'Tis not by word Thy love is shown,--
A priceless Gift was given,
When Jesus left the Father's throne,
And stooped to earth from heaven;--
My God, to Thee my praise I bring,
For Thou hast taught my soul to sing.

IV

Thus shall my praise be comely, Lord,
And like Thy love divine,
When gift shall far surpass my word,
And life with praise combine;--
My God, to Thee my praise I bring,
For Thou hast taught my soul to sing.

Rev. John Brownlie, D.D.

MEDITATIONS XI
tr., John Brownlie
8.6.8.6

I

The Lord is very good to those
Who seek His matchless grace;
The needy find supplies in Him,
The weak a resting-place.

II

The Lord is very good to those
Who own His sovereign Will;--
A path of safety is for such
As His commands fulfil.

III

Who hope in God in light and dark,
In failure and success,
Enjoy a bliss surpassing far
Earth's utmost blessedness.

IV

And they who seek the love of God
May fear no earthly frown;
For nought of earth can quench the flame
That waters cannot drown.

V

O Jesus Christ! in Thee we trust,
And rest upon Thy care;
In mercy, then, Thy mercy send,
In answer to our prayer.

VI
Now, unto Christ, the Blessed Son,
And God with Whom He dwells,
And to the Holy Paraclete,
Be glory that excels.

MEDITATIONS XII
tr., John Brownlie
he ph'lanthropia tou Patros.

I

The pity of the Father,
The kindness of the Son,
The comfort of the Spirit,--
Immortal Three in One;
All high and low, in heaven and earth,
Proclaim in songs of holy mirth.

II

When earth was dark and cheerless,
And mankind hopeless pined,
A thought of pity, peerless,
'Woke in the Father's mind;
And lo! the Word to man was given,
That spake to earth the thought of heaven.

III

The Son all condescending
Came from the heart of God,
And heaven and earth were blending,
Where'er the God-man trod;
He sought the erring souls to win
From straying in the ways of sin.

IV

And when the work was ended,
And Christ to God returned,
The Holy Ghost descended
In cloven tongues that burned;
He took the words of Christ again,
And spake them to the hearts of men.

Rev. John Brownlie, D.D.

V

Now unto God be glory,
And unto Christ the Son,
And to the Blessed Spirit--
Immortal Three in One;
All high and low in heaven and earth,
Proclaim in songs of holy mirth.

MEDITATIONS XIII
tr., John Brownlie
pistos ho theos.

I

I have no other thought but this,
That Thou wilt faithful prove;
For Thou didst give Thyself, O Christ,
In Thy abundant love.

II

For not alone the word, O God,
In burning letters came;
The Word Incarnate dwelt with us,
And wore our human name.

III

Who can the grace of God deny,
To whom the Gift is given?
Or doubt the love of Christ for man,
Who came for man from heaven?

IV

O love of God, surpassing great!
Who would not trust its power,
But doubt the faithfulness of God,
In every needy hour?

V

I have no other thought but this,
That Thou wilt faithful prove;
For Thou didst give Thyself, O Christ,
In Thy abundant love.

MEDITATIONS XIV
tr., John Brownlie

I

Hear me, O Lord, in mercy hear,
And let my prayer like incense rise;
My spirit feels Thy presence near,
And rests upon Thy Sacrifice.

II

I have no need Thou can'st not meet,
There is no want that I can crave,
But, lo! I find it at Thy feet,
O Christ, Who cam'st my life to save.

III

'Tis pardon, Lord, my soul desires;
And cleansing, most of all, I need;
The strength the Holy Ghost inspires,
His joy to cheer, His light to lead.

IV

That I may serve Thee as I ought,
And do Thy will from day to day;
Help me to live as Thou hast taught,
And grant the grace for which I pray.

V

O, I am poor, and weak, and blind--
My soul is empty and distressed;
But, Lord, I have the earnest mind,
And with Thy blessing, would be blest.

MEDITATIONS XV
tr., John Brownlie

I

Open to me the gates of lovingkindness,
Laden and sin-stained let me enter in;
Pity my weakness, and my guilty blindness,
Free me in mercy from the thrall of sin.

II

Give me to know that, in Thy grace abounding,
Thou hast forgiveness for the sin-sick soul;
That, by Thy love my waywardness surrounding,
Thou can'st allure me to Thy sweet control.

III

Say to my soul, when doubt and fear assailing,
Curtain the light that from Thy presence flows,
Thine is a power, O Jesus Christ, prevailing
Over the threatening of life's countless woes.

IV

Jesus, Who came, and on the Cross of sadness,
Bore in Thy weakness all my sin and shame;
Change Thou for me my sorrow into gladness,
Give me to glory in Thy matchless name.

V

Open to me the gates of lovingkindness,
Laden and sin-stained, I would enter in;
Pity my weakness, and my guilty blindness,
Free me in mercy from the thrall of sin.

MEDITATIONS XVI
tr., John Brownlie

I

When clouds obscure the rising sun,
And darkness weeps where joy should sing;
Hail, then, my soul, the day begun,
And wait the light that noon shall bring.

II

If clouds like curtains veil the light,
When day at noon should brightly smile;
Up, then, my soul, it is not night,
The glory tarries but a while.

III

Wait till the hills that bar the west--
That pierce the clouds their summits crown--
Snatch, ere the day declines to rest,
The glory as the sun goes down.

IV

More bright than morn, than noon more fair,
The purple and the gold serene;
The light and rapture everywhere,
That sing, and shine, the clouds between.

V

If waits the joy of God betimes,
And tears bedew where smiles should be;
If dark the noon when sunlight climbs,
The light at eve thine eyes shall see.

VARIOUS I
tr., John Brownlie
ergo Soter mou deiknueis, hoti su ei he panton anastasis.
From the Office of the Burial of a Priest

I

Thou art our Resurrection,
O Jesus Christ the Lord;
Who call'st the dead from hades,
By Thy commanding word;

II

Then fetters strong are sundered,
And prison gates undone;
And light illumes the darkness
As by the rising sun.

III

Thou from the grave at Beth'ny,
When wept the sisters twain,
Didst raise the mourned-for brother,
Whom death had ruthless slain.

IV

'Twas from a sleep Thou call'dst him,
As when the daylight breaks,
And morning whispers gently,
And man from slumber wakes.

V

O gentle name to give it--
"He is not dead but sleeps"--
For death has no dominion,
O'er those whom Jesus keeps.

Rev. John Brownlie, D.D.

VI

Thou art our Resurrection,
O Jesus Christ the Lord;
And Thou from sleep wilt bring us,
According to Thy word.

VII
All glory, laud, and honour,
To Jesus Christ be given,
By mortals and immortals,
Who dwell in earth and heaven.

VARIOUS II
tr., John Brownlie
alethos mataiotes ta sumpanta ho de bios skia kai enupnion.
From the Office of the Burial of a Priest

I

Vain are the things of time,
Our life a passing dream;
A shadow flitting in the sun,
A leaf upon the stream;
Lord, in Thy faithful keeping,
Rest Thou Thy servant sleeping.

II

Seek we the world in vain,
Vainly we clutch the prize,
And sink into the lonesome grave,
Where prince with beggar lies;
Lord, in Thy faithful keeping,
Rest Thou Thy servant sleeping.

III

Rest Thou Thy servant, Lord,
Whose earthly task is done;
Who can no longer hear the call
To toil beneath the sun;
Lord, in Thy faithful keeping,
Rest Thou Thy servant sleeping.

IV

Lord, with Thy gentle ones,
In glory's dwelling-place,
Receive Thy servant whom we mourn,
Who served Thee by Thy grace;
Lord, in Thy faithful keeping,
Rest Thou Thy servant sleeping.

Rev. John Brownlie, D.D.

V

We would not weep for those
Who in Thy faith depart;
For thou, O Christ, dost bear them hence,
And bind them to Thy heart;
Lord, in Thy faithful keeping,
Rest Thou Thy servant sleeping.

VARIOUS III
tr., John Brownlie
kurie, anapauson to nepion.
From the Office of the Burial of a Child

I

Lord, rest the child; cut off at morning hour,
Crushed as a bud before it came to flower;
Gone as the star that lent its feeble ray,
Ere yet the morn had brightened into day.

II

Lord, rest the child; no bliss on earth was thine,
Drink now the pleasures of the life divine;
Here streams that gladden, when the sun is high,
Shrink in their channels, 'neath a burning sky.

III

Lord, rest the child; within the heavenly place,
Thine angel ever views the Father's face;
Thine is the kingdom, and to claim His own,
Christ left the glory of a kingly throne.

IV

Lord, rest the child; we will not weep for thee--
Death is not death to those with Christ that be;
Mourn we with weeping, that the sin is ours,
To blight the beauty of earth's fairest flowers.

VARIOUS IV
tr., John Brownlie
From the Office for Baptism

I

Bear to the font the child of grace,
And there the sacred rite attend,
Whose healing virtues can efface
The stains that to the soul extend.

II

There, as at Jordan long ago,
The heavenly Dove in power descends;
New life in fulness to bestow,
And grace that on the life attends.

III

Christ, let Thy blood in freeness spilt,
This water fitly symbolise;
And all the vileness and the guilt,
Be laid upon Thy Sacrifice.

IV

And let the sacred sign he wears,
Adorn the inner life, we pray;
Till every word, and action bears,
The impress of that Cross alway.

V

Come to our aid, O Spirit true;
Hearts with Thy living truth inspire;
And to our languid souls renew
The love that wakes responsive fire.

VARIOUS V

tr., John Brownlie
eleous pege, huparchon Huperagathe.
From the Order of Holy Unction

I

A Fount of mercy, Lord, Thou art,
Perennial and Divine;
The source of every lasting good,
And every grace is Thine;
Now to the suffering healing give,
And touch the sick that he may live.

II

O Saviour, Thou alone art God,
And Thou art quick to heal;
For Thou didst wear our feeble flesh,
And all our ailments feel;
And Thou canst make the sufferer whole,
And save the sin afflicted soul.

III

O Christ, the Great Physician Thou,
Tender and full of power;
Now with the oil of grace anoint
The sufferer at this hour;--
Bid Thou the pain and weakness cease,
And give the sore afflicted peace.

VARIOUS VI
tr., John Brownlie
Christos mou dunamis.
At the Departure of a Soul

I

O God, most good, forget me not--
Nor from Thy servant turn away--
Who to the night of death hast brought
My fearful soul this awful day.

II

Hear Thou my prayer, O God of grace,
Who every penitent receives;
From memory let my tears efface,
The sin for which my spirit grieves.

III

O ye, my kinsfolk, brethren, friends,
Your weeping mingle with mine own;
My soul the dire behest attends,
And wings its flight from earth alone.

IV

Now none can save, and nought can aid:
Be Thou mine aid, O Christ my God,
Lest I for evermore be laid,
Beneath the all-avenging rod.

VARIOUS VII
tr., John Brownlie
At the Departure of a Soul

I

Death's dark and moonless night,
Me, unprepared, o'ertakes;
Lord, send Thy mercy while my soul
Its fearful journey makes;
Let not a spirit of dismay
Depress me on the awful way.

II

Lo, vain my life hath been,
And full of deadly cares;
Now these prevent my anxious soul,
And lay their bitter snares;
Let not a spirit of dismay
Depress me on the awful way.

III

The number of my sins,
Lord, let it not exceed
The fulness of Thy mercy great,
To overtake my need;
Nor let a spirit of dismay
Depress me on the awful way.

IV

For now they lead me hence,--
They gird me round about;
Rebellion stirs within my soul,
'Mid awful pangs of doubt;--
Let not a spirit of dismay
Depress me on the awful way.

Rev. John Brownlie, D.D.

V

In my affliction, Lord,
No comfort can I find;
Be Thou my comfort in my woe,
Who art exceeding kind;
Let not a spirit of dismay
Depress me on the awful way.

VARIOUS VIII
tr., John Brownlie

I

O Light of lights around my pathway shining,
Brighter than day;
Sun of my soul, Thy orb hath no declining,
No lessening ray;--
No solemn twilight tells of coming night,
Thou art eternal noon, O Light of light.

II

Blind in the night, I vainly sighed and sorrowed,
Groping for day;
Cheer from the borrowed light of earth I borrowed,
That died away;
But morning dawned, O glorious and bright,
And Thou hast filled my soul, O Light of light.

III

Bright be Thy beams when other lights are dying,
Light from on high;
Laden with joy, when earthly joys are lying
Withered and dry;--
Light of my life, my joy in earthly sorrow,
Chase Thou the gloom, and bring the glad to-morrow.

Rev. John Brownlie, D.D.

APPENDIX

A copy of the draft of The Church of Scotland Mission Hymn Book, compiled by a committee, and sanctioned by last General Assembly for publication, has come into the writer's hands, too late to be collated for the foregoing Table. The Hymn Book, which is intended for use at Mission services--both those of a permanent Mission, and those of Mission-weeks, including Guild, and Missionary, and other special services, for which The Church Hymnary and The Scottish Hymnal do not make sufficient provision--contains 338 hymns, and 18 metrical Psalms and Paraphrases, all of which, so far as one can judge from a casual survey, and without the music, seem suitable for the purpose to which the book will be devoted. The noteworthy particular in connection with this Collection, and that which demands this reference to it, is the fact that, here for the first time in the history of Scottish hymnody, we have something approaching a satisfactory representation of hymns from the Greek; and it is not lacking in significance that the book to include so many, should be a Mission Hymn Book. No one who has studied Scottish hymnody will miss the significance of this fact. If the Greek Church, which is variously characterised by its critics, be a non-missionary Church, it can at least supply hymns, if not for the ordinary services of the sanctuary, then for Mission services. Such, at any rate, would seem to be the conviction of the compilers of The Mission Hymn Book. The thirteen hymns from the Greek contained in this book, the first lines of which are given below, include three which are presented for use for the first time, viz., (g) (i) (n), increasing the number of Greek hymns in common use from forty-one (as shewn by the Table on pages 20-23) to forty-four.

(a) Art thou weary, art thou languid?
    (Based upon the Greek) tr. Dr. Neale.
(b) Behold the Bridegroom cometh
    (Midnight Office) tr. G. Moultrie.
(c) Christian, dost thou see them?
    (St. Andrew of Crete) tr. Dr. Neale.
(d) Far from Thy heavenly care
    (St. Joseph of the Studium) tr. Dr. Brownlie.
(e) God of all grace, Thy mercy send
    (Litany of the Deacon) tr. Dr. Brownlie.
(f) O brightness of the Eternal Father's face
    (Sophronius) tr. E. W. Eddis.
(g) O may my soul, uncrushed by care
    (Synesius) tr. Dr. Brownlie.
(h) O Saviour, in Thy pitying grace
    (Theoctistus) tr. R. M. Moorsom.
(i) Our hearts to heaven uprising

(Morning service, Horologion) tr. Dr. Brownlie.
(k) Safe home, safe home in port
 (Based upon the Greek) tr. Dr. Neale.
(l) Stars of the morning
 (St. Joseph) tr. Dr. Neale.
(m) Those eternal bowers
 (St. John of Damascus) tr. Dr. Neale.
(n) When glory crowned the mountain top
 (Based upon the Greek) tr. Dr. Brownlie.

www.ingramcontent.com/pod-product-compliance
Lightning Source LLC
Chambersburg PA
CBHW032007080426
42735CB00007B/529